DEGAS

THIS VOLUME, EDITED BY

ANDRÉ GLOECKNER

WAS FIRST PUBLISHED IN OCTOBER MCMXXXVII
BY THE HYPERION PRESS, PARIS. COLOUR
BLOCKS ENGRAVED BY ÉTABLISSEMENTS JEAN
MALVAUX, BRUSSELS; COLOUR PLATES AND
TEXT PRINTED BY IMPRIMERIE J.-E. GOOSSENS;
PHOTOGRAVURES PRINTED BY SOC. AN. DE
ROTOGRAVURE; BINDING BY A. MEERSMANS,
BRUSSELS.

DEGAS

BY

CAMILLE MAUCLAIR

Sole Agents for the United States
FRENCH AND EUROPEAN PUBLICATIONS INC.
610, FIFTH AVENUE, NEW-YORK

PARIS

THE HYPERION PRESS

#1421938

EDGAR DEGAS

THAT an artist should be both celebrated and inadequately known is not very unusual, for creative originality ever retains some of its secrets. But in the case of Degas it would seem that the artist and the man, in their aggressive independance, agreed to hoodwink each other, and take a singular pleasure in the inexactitude of the judgments of the critics and those of the public. During the twenty years since the death of this great creator we have incessantly corrected, by successive cross-checks, opinions which were dictated to us through admiration : and we still continue to admire more and more, but the works and its author appear to us, if not less mysterious, at least different from what we believed to be certain. We have gone astray as regards Degas and his character, the meaning of his work and their position in the French School of painting. In this short study I would endeavour to show, apart from what he was, what he was erroneously accounted to be.

He was born in Paris, in the Rue Saint-Georges, on June 19, 1834. He detested his christian name of Edgar, and, considering that the use of the nobiliary particle of his family name, De Gas, was puerile, he signed himself plain « Degas ». His father came of an ancient Breton stock, but was born in Naples; his mother belonged to the Musson family, which several generations before had emigrated to New Orleans, where it amassed a considerable fortune. This mingled aristocratic and middle-class heredity influenced the moral formation of the cold, defiant, and caustic youth in whose eyes femininity hardly existed and who was ruled by only one passion, — that for drawing. Classical studies (which in those days were serious) he pursued willingly; he even attended courses at the School of Law. And then he declared his vocation.

He was able to devote himself to his profession without material cares, and no obstacle whatsoever was placed in his way. He entered the Ecole des Beaux-Arts in 1855. He was then a pale-faced young man, — that dull pallor reminding people of the maternal Creole strain in his blood; and his face, enframed by thick brown hair, possessed almost sunken eyes that were interrogative, pensive, and sad, forming a striking contrast with the strong sensual lips of the mouth and a determined chin. Reticence, obstinacy, disdain, and restrained violence, — that is what we see in the first portrait (in addition to an etching) we possess of him by himself : a strong and gloomy work garnered by the Louvre. Making but a transitory stay at the Ecole des Beaux-Arts, he sought from Lamothe, the pupil of Hippolyte Flandrin, a recollection of Ingres' teaching; became intimate with Elie Delaunay; and then went to Italy.

When in Rome he became the friend of Bonnat, Paul Dubois, and Chapu, who were going through their course of instruction at the Villa Médecis. Later such friendships considerably surprised those who took Degas to be an Impressionnist revolutionary. He also knew Georges Bizet and Gustave Moreau. Death alone severed these intimate relationships. Degas, reputed to be insensitive and even disagreeable, ever remained faithful to them, though he did not check his flashes of wit. In Tuscany he devoted himself whole-heartedly to drawing, either landscapes or, especially, the copying of works by masters of the XIVth century : analysizing them shrewdly and, with a tenacious care for perfection, searching for himself in their works. Poussin also influenced him. With masterly hand he copied his *Rape of the Sabines;* whilst Ingres, whose works he was also to copy later on, indicated to him what he believed was his true course, — portraiture and historical compositions.

Consequently, on his return, Degas undertook simultaneously the production of historical pictures and the completion of a large portrait begun in Florence at the house of his uncle, the Senator Baron Bellelli, and depicting him in his home with his wife and two daughters. This work, which the artist showed to no one and which remained unknown until after his death, contains some very fine features and bears witness to considerable effort : it is severe, somewhat frigid, and wholly classical. Degas was dissatisfied with it and discouraged. Never again did he undertake such groups of similar dimensions; but, fortunately for us, he did not renounce those isolated figures which, with some masterpieces, have raised him to the rank of the finest psychological portraitists of our School.

As regards historical compositions, from 1860 to 1865, he attempted them with such works as *Young Spartans wrestling, Jephthah's Daughter, Semiramis building a Town, The Misfortunes of the City of Orleans, Alexander and Bucephalus;* and these also have stupefied a generation which discovered Impressionism and ranked the Degas identified with pictures of dancing-girls, women in their baths, and race-course scenes with the new movement. Above all the artist was seeking, with the utmost integrity, for the association of skilful lines and the solution of problems of a technical order. He was linked to classicism. They admitted him to the Salon, though quietly : the jury appreciated the science and nicety of his draughtsmanship, and hoped that he would become an eminent historical painter. But suddenly he abandoned that path. Was he weary of his subjects — freely chosen though they were? Was he disturbed by the paradox between Ingres, whom he adored, and Delacroix, whom he admired, and did he fear to come to grief by trying to conciliate them, as was to happen to his comrade Gustave Moreau, — less fortunate than Chassériau? Implacably clear-sighted as he was, did he recognize that, born to express the truth, he lacked imagination? Perhaps that was the deep reason. He wrote nothing and said hardly anything about himself, so we can merely conjecture.

At that time, Degas, some thirty years of age, associated with the group of naturalist painters and novelists who assembled at the Café Guerbois, in the Batignolles quarter of Paris, to establish — tumultuously — the principles of a new aestheticism. They were in agreement as to the necessity of « being true » to life, each after his own fashion and temperament, but in a common revolt against academic teachings and false literary idealism. Zola and Manet were the most remarkable and most combative figures of this movement, at whose meetings men like Claude Monet, Renoir, Legros, Fantin-Latour, and Stevens were on friendly terms with mere Bohemians, — and with the latter the correct, reserved, and sarcastic Degas had absolutely nothing in common. He listened in silence and fought shy of theories. But from that time onwards his name was connected with these men, and he began to receive his share of the furious attacks directed against them. He accepted, out of sympathy for these so-called outcasts and through his own love of independance, the ostracism doubly provoked by this new associates and his desertion of those followers of historical painting who had counted on him as a brilliant recruit. He was hardly a « naturalist » in the sense that word was used by the frequenters of the Café Guerbois, and he was to become still less an « impressionist » at the time of the invention of that term eight or nine years later. Yet he was so catalogued almost up to our own days.

Nevertheless he exhibited with his new friends and despite the fact that he was often opposed to their tendencies. He had the courage and the delicacy to claim his share of insults, — he who was so disdainful of hubbub and ostentation, who loved nothing so much as work in silence, and who, like Manet, had a care for personal elegance and good form. But he possessed his own idea of realism, and never believed in the new dogma of « do nothing save in the presence of nature and in the open air », — a dogma which seemed to him to be both puerile and inconsistant. What influenced him most at this period of uncertainty was Japanese art as revealed to him by the engraver Bracquemond. Hokusai's magic line made him glimpse the possibility of uniting to that of the Primitives, Adnet, and Ingres a new expression of modern subjects. And when he had carried out his duty of friendship with his accursed comrades, he abstained from their private shows as well as the Salon, and no longer exhibited his works save on very rare occasions, at the Durand-Ruel Gallery, since he had no need to sell his pictures for a livelihood and held what was called renown and honour in derision. Slowly and as it were in an occult manner, his glory was built up among an élite, — almost despite himself. What had been mistaken for misanthropy was the effect of a most noble and lofty conception of the independance of the artist who reserves all his faculties for his work and surrenders all vanities for the sake of his art.

In 1873, Degas went on a journey to New Orléans to see his uncle Musson and his brothers, Achille and René, who were wealthy cotton-merchants. And he depicted them in their office, on a celebrated canvas which, with its clear and frigid precision, worthy of a little Dutch master, is really in no way impressionistic. Furthermore, he ever remained on good terms with his family, as witness the portraits of his girl cousin, his father, and his relatives, the Duke and Duchess Morbilli. But this sojourn in America does not appear to have had any more influence upon him than his long tours in Morocco and Spain, accompanied by Boldini, his Belgian and Dutch excursions, and his visits to Pausilippo, where his family had a villa. Paris alone captivated him, apart from a few weeks rest in the Orne. He lived the life of a bourgeois, more and more confined to his studio, seeing only a few rare friends, and consenting to dine in town on the strict condition that it was without ceremony and that he was to be entirely at his ease.

As early as 1865 he had chosen his subjects : the racing and dancing worlds, and at the same time portraits, to be followed by feminine nudes. But he visited the race-courses merely in order to observe and exercise his prodigious optical memory, to satisfy his passion for movement, and then to record it with the exactitude of the still unforeseen cinematographic camera. The same reason directed his steps to the Opera : first of all to the orchestra, for, like his god M. Ingres, he loved music and had become intimate with the instrumentalists, notably with the bassoonist Dihau and his sister, to whom he presented admirable portraits; then behind the scenes and into the choreographic « salles d'étude », where he discovered inexhaustible material for his inspired mania for drawing. Only later was all this known, after the well-to-do painter (like Manet, the fashionable man-about-town) had been taken for a dilettante of « la pelouse » and the stage, whilst the academic crowd deplored that this « hope » of theirs had turned out badly and spoilt his talent, — nay, degraded it by seeking for subjects at the « café-concert », if not, sometimes, in brothels, and thus in anticipation of Forain and Lautrec. In reality, Degas was searching everywhere for movement and line; mere subjects interested him less and less, as well as the concept of beauty, for which he substituted that of character.

People called him a realist; but he was really preaching an antiliterary, almost abstract art. The man who was thought to be a revolutionary was a middle-class conservative of the old stock. We can well understand how all this confused the opinions of a generation which, at last acclaiming impressionism, ranked Degas side by side with Manet, Renoir, or Monet, on the faith of dates and controversies. That generation formed a very false idea, and then, when better informed, bore the old recluse a grudge for not having resembled it. On the other hand, he had lost contact with the post-impressionists, and when he saw the first works of the « fauves », he did not conceal his contempt; and thus brought down upon him the rancour of their critics. He worked as long as was physically possible. His sight declining, progressively, he became almost blind. Whereupon he struggled to produce for himself alone works of an entirely new style, in which colour, until then a secondary consideration, assumed the primary rôle, with strange vividness, on a form he could no longer perceive. Once more he set to work to model, with fumbling fingers, a few statues, at one and the same time strange and admirable. Then all was over. The livelong day Degas wandered about the streets of Paris, — the very image, as one of his friends has said, of ancient Homer. The war of 1914 brought him to the verge of despair. He died in anguish on September 26, 1917, at the age of eighty-three. Amidst a multitude of deaths, his passing aroused little attention. The painter — a stay-at-home bachelor, deprived of all official honours, which, moreover, he never desired — passed away unobtrusively, despite the glory which came to him so tardily.

Many of his witty remarks have been quoted. They have gained for him the reputation of having been a bitter-tongued hypochondriac, and, indeed, his words were often cruel. But they were always just and inspired only by those who were vain, insincere, or mediocre. It is also well to point out that many people have attributed to the old artist their own rancorous and disparaging utterances. Degas' observations, in their lapidary form, can be authenticated by something approaching profundity, by their rare critical quality, and incisiveness. To note a few of them will not be unprofitable. Gustave Moreau's predilection for over-loading his academic nudes with precious stones drew from Degas, despite his friendship, the words : « He adornes the Apollo Belvidere with a watch-chain ». The same painter affected to live in a mystic retreat, but this did not prevent him becoming a member of the Institute and professor at the Ecole des Beaux-Arts, and from selling his pictures at a very high price. « He is a hermit, but well-acquainted with the railway time-table », remarked Degas. There, in two little sketches, is Moreau depicted in his entirety. Apropos of a slovenly-dressed and dirty painter who, having been decorated with the cross of the Legion of Honour, went from café to café to show off his red ribbon, Degas exclaimed : « Well, that is merely one more stain on his person ».

On another occasion, whilst Degas was silently studying the pictures in a flashy picture-show, the exhibitor persisted on being introduced to him. « Did you paint these pictures, Monsieur? » enquired Degas. « Certainly, Maître », replied the delighted artist... Whereupon Degas was heard to mutter : « I am sorry for you! » as he walked away. In front of a picture depicting a charge of cuirassiers, Degas exclaimed : « They are fleeing from Detaille ». When a picture which he had formerly sold for five hundred francs fetched at auction more than 400,000 francs, reporters came to ask him for his impressions. « My impressions », he replied, « are those of the horse which, having won the Grand Prix, receives merely his ordinary feed of oats. Moreover, I do not think that the author of this picture is an idiot; but the person who paid so dear for it is certainly one ». Finally, it was Degas who, to a young painter who was boasting to him of his success, made this dignified and admirable reply : « In my time, Monsieur, we did not *get on* ». Assuredly these are redoubtable sallies, but they were prompted more by a love of truth and a passion for art than by malignity, and there has not been placed on record either the admirable reflections which the old master uttered on the subject of masterpieces, or the many kindly acts he was unable to hide, — and so much so did he hide them that intimate friends like Forain, Boldini, Mary Cassatt, and Zuloaga have refrained from bearing witness to them. Fundamentally his life was a very secret one. He did everything he could to put us off the track of its real significance; and possibly a youthful love affair, ending in disappointment, was the aggravating cause of a melancholy nature, hidden under his sarcastic disdain. Certain poems — for he turned to poesy for his own pleasure — lead out thoughts in that direction...

It has been surmised and repeated that Degas, devoted to historical painting, was suddenly, and for some unknown reason, converted to realism and modernism, after the manner of Manet and the Goncourt brothers rather than that of Zola. The explanation of his second period is not to be found there. It may be that the artist, apt in the lucid analysis of himself as of others, noted the insufficiency of his imagination. It may also be that he was sensitive to the influence of the circle into which, when rebuffed by those of the academic school, he penetrated, — and still more sensitive may he have been to the revelation of Japanese art. But Degas was too subtle, too innately aristocratic, — although he asserted himself to be a bourgeois, — to confine himself to naturalism pure and simple. The key to his art was his passion for draughtsmanship, — the drawing of things « in movement ». Beyond mere subjects, which were to interest him less and less, it was first of all linear combination which attracted him, — that of planes and masses obsessing him only later; it was, above all, his ambition to attain the very boundary of the expression of truth, that which responded to the depths of his nature, but a truth which did not exclude decorative fancy and an unforeseen presentation, as opposed to a flat and short-sighted copy of details.

From that moment of his life, Degas detached himself from the Ingresque conception of the beautiful in itself : he remained faithful to his admiration for the Primitives, who attached themselves to character as to a stable notion, dominating what is arbitrarily called ugliness and beauty. And above all was he a draughtsman, limiting himself, in so far as a painter, to deep colour-scales in portraiture, light and sobre ones in landscape, with a few high-lights. Polychromy made but a weak appeal to him, and, whilst appreciating the magnificent gifts of a Claude Monet, he considered that to sacrifice everything in the pursuit of fugitive effects of the sun was an error, — that light was only one of the elements of composition, of which an artist ought to be not the slave but the master, — and that the atmosphere of great masterpieces had no need to be breathable.

He declared to intimate friends : « No art is less spontaneous than mine, which is wholly reflective ». And also this, which it ill became him to understand clearly : « *You* need life in its natural, *I* in its artificial form ». By this he meant that art begins when one ponders over, re-composes, or dissociates to one's taste what life has presented to the eye. All this is from the mouth of a classicist. It was only later that Degas, a marvellous harmonist, was to give greater importance to the charming skill of the colourist, — nay, he was to give it a preponderance when form began to fade away before his menaced eyes. Furthermore he never ceased to unite closely tonality, volume, line, etc., when so many artists have seen paradoxes therein and have felt themselves obliged to choose between colour or design, as on the occasion of the Ingres-Delacroix duel. Degas admired the latter without ceasing to admire the former.

It was natural that, when Degas relinquished historical or legendary themes in order to direct his attention to daily life, he should satisfy his passion for drawing, — and the drawing of things in movement, — by studying the race-course world. « Modern subjects », « open air subjects », but above all subjects enabling him to study the attitude of animals and fix their instability. He has placed his scenes of the turf amidst true and pleasant landscapes, painted with a light touch, and people were able to see, at the Durand-Ruel Gallery, almost furtively and when the artist was about sixty years of age, a series of magnificent little evocations of nature (watercolours, oil-paintings, or pastels, without a single figure) which proved his mastery in that branch of art. But he was distrustful of the « plein air », and, after the fashion of a true classicist regarded landscapes merely as a document for the studio, not as an end in itself, — a restriction which completely isolated him from the Barbizon painters and the Impressionists. What attracted him was the study of horses snorting or galloping, alone or in groups : their musculature, well-proportioned lines, and arabesque formation. He noted their shining cruppers, the hue and value of their shadows on the ground, the colouring of their bodies in the sun-light, but especially their linear combinations, the unexpectedness of their instantaneity, with an audacious veracity which only photography, raised to an art, has been able to equal in our time.

On these horses, or near them, are jockeys, trainers, and backers, seen in their professional attitudes, and enhanced with a charm which no negative could record, — the charm of Degas' enthusiasm and incisive spirit. These pictures, as far distant from the frigid minuteness of a Meissonier as they are from the amusing yet summary confusion of spots of colour of the Impressionists, these light and silvery pictures, with here and there a few most tactfully distributed touches of a beautiful black and brilliant high-lights would have inspired a Boldini or a Berthe Morisot equally well. They are not only marvels of anatomy and observation of life, so much so that no one ever placed a man better on his horse, which he directs by hardly perceptible pressure, and with which he forms but a single being, at one and the same time thick-set and light; they also witness to Degas' intense desire to inscribe within his frames a wholly new setting, which at that time appeared to be paradoxical and even provocative, whereas, disdaining any wish to astonish, the artist found pretexts in nature herself and in those decorative combinations which the lines and values of creatures moving amidst immobile surroundings offer.

This originality in composition, — not arbitrarily intentional, but recommended by a sense of veracity to a man who knew how to observe and retain, — was to be one of Degas' cares, up to the point of becoming an obsession and at times an ironical affectation, when people took exception to his way of placing a woman's face almost behind a large vase, or, in an angle, side by side with an enormous bouquet, — things which, sixty years ago, scandalized the public as much as a frankly blue shadow in a landscape, though one could see them every day. But it is the characteristic of great painters to teach us to observe more accurately, and no one in our time will be found to have contributed to this more than the independant and solitary Degas.

Everything is understood, everything well considered in this art of his, prepared after the most serious classical studies, whereas contemporaries saw in it principally « realistic and modernistic » subjects, « slices of life » by a skilful artist who had renounced the conventional ideal of the Ecole. At the same time, Degas transformed his technique, which up to then was somewhat bald, merely accentuating and enhancing the drawing. For a smooth pigment he substituted thicker paint laid on with juxtaposed and broader touches; he began to search for contour, less by means of the Ingresque line than by modelling, creating a limitation of form, no longer from the outside but the inside; and above all became enamoured of pastel, which he was to employ sometimes by hatching as in the final works of Chardin, sometimes with a thousand refinements as regards treatment, or the choice of papers, so much so that he became not only the premier pastellist of our time but one of the greatest with La Tour and Perronneau. And it was with such an arm that he attacked his considerable series of *Dancing-girls*, or rather their double life, on and off the stage.

Long had he gazed upon them from the orchestra, when sketching or painting his musical friends, in the semi-darkness of their pit, above which, beyond the footlights, shone the stage illuminations, the illusory wizardry of opera and ballet. How frequently he aroused astonishment — nay, even indignation — by placing in the foreground, as a black value against a luminous ground, the scroll of a double-bass, or by showing in perspective, at the top of the picture, only the legs and the « sticking out » skirts of the ballet-dancers. His sole object was to refine on the contrast between that luminous zone and the blacks and whites of dress-coats and shirt-fronts. But soon this picturesqueness no longer satisfied him. A regular attendant in this special world, he came to understand both its seductive factitiousness and hidden wretchedness. A passion for truth possessed him. He was seized with a desire to get to the bottom of things, and explain what these chrysalids, which the public mistook to be butterflies, really were.

This close observer — incapable of grouping imaginary figures, but capable of arbitrarily re-composing and re-associating the elements of real life — was struck by the contrast between the enchanting illusion of choreography and the hard work it entailed, and to which the public never gave a thought. He took a pleasure, pictorially, in the sometimes strange effects of artificial light on flesh and materials, though the Opera house in his day was devoid of all our present-day resources and the multitudinous services now rendered by electricity. There can be no doubt that the analysis of those artificial lightings largely contributed to his evolution towards the predominance of colouring, after his severe manner and his cult for the line of Ingres, Holbein, or the last of the Primitives, until in the end colour, or rather the power of highly coloured values, shattered, as it were, the armature of the drawing in his last works.

But he discovered still another lure of the theatre which turned out to be a beautiful lie : the human reality of the below-stage world. It was not the celebrated, wealthy, and fêted ballet-girls who interested him, but the poor little plebeians of the « corps de ballet », representing the unknown and sorrowful reverse of illusion. And not only did he pass from the auditorium to the wings, — he entered the bare, light, and cold rooms where these young girls of the « faubourg » were trained. They came there from their wretched lodgings, sometimes conducted by a « Madame Cardinal », such as his friend Ludovic Halévy depicted, sometimes alone, girls already vicious and even devoted to harlotry. Their salaries were poor; their work exceedingly hard. Physical exercices disarticulated their ill-nourished young bodies, from which an excessive muscular effort was demanded. A thankless profession indeed! — and one which those adolescent girls chose more in the hope of meeting some serious « entreteneur » than of securing leading rôles in the limelight, and finally attaining to the glory of a « star ». At the same time as acrobatics they were taught to be elegant, graceful, and stylish, for they were of the « lower orders », and remained so both in speech and manners as soon as they were at rest, as soon as their master had stopped beating time with his big stick for the steps repeated a hundred times, and the fiddler had ceased scraping on his instrument to guide them. These disciplinary lessons, at which fines were levied, were a thorough preparation for first-night performances.

Degas looked on and listened. He conversed with these little dancing-girls. He noted everything : their obscene, or naïve remarks as well as their wretched personal linen, their cast-off clothing, and dancing-sandals. In his insatiable passion for truth he experienced a bitter satisfaction. His irony took on a keener edge; and at the same time his heart was filled with pity for that « chair à plaisir » served up for the amusement of comfortable bourgeois, who feasted their eyes upon it through their opera-glasses. « Sous le fouet du plaisir, ce bourreau sans merci... » — (Beneath the scourge of pleasure, this merciless executioner...) Our thoughts wander to Baudelaire, he who was also both sarcastic and touched to the heart; to Baudelaire whom Degas perhaps never read. In any case Degas would have been horrified at the idea of producing « literary » paintings. But he was a man, both secretly good and infinitely sensitive.

So he sketched and painted these girls, with faces almost invariably vulgar, or ugly; limbs heavily-jointed; bosoms flat or prematurely wizened, — all to undergo a complete transformation through their make-up, tawdry finery, and stage perspective. In their company he satisfied at one and the same time his appetite for truth and his mania for movement. Each girl was insignificant in herself, merely one of the scattered units of a great piece of mechanism — the ballet. A signal, a few notes, and they assembled to form a composite whole and live a special, unusual life, in which creatures became other than they were, amidst an atmosphere as artificial as themselves. Degas knew them, summoned them to his studio, analysed them in a multitude of sketches, seized on the wing the scenic attitudes at his request. Then he returned to witness their rehearsals and, relying on his notebook, as little intelligible to the profane as hieroglyphics, he observed how those isolated figures came together to form the arabesques of their incessantly united and disunited groups.

They were no longer women, salaried figurants, but rythmic elements, figure combinations. How were all these bodies to be combined, what was to be done with these arms and legs, multitudinous pistils of flesh issuing from flower-cups of coloured muslin, living bouquets in movement, snow-flakes flitting on the stage? What a joy it was to Degas to wrestle with these complex problems, added to which was the difficulty of the fugative transposition of tonalities in the strong illumination of evenings at the Opera! Baudelarian bitterness was no longer in question. If Degas' thoughts strayed to the poets, at that period of his work, they drew near rather to the way in which his friend Mallarmé viewed the ballet and its artificiality. Not at all! — he was a painter, with never a thought save for his draughtsmanship, combined with tonalities indissolubly. And thus he produced his marvellous charcoal drawings touched up with pastel, resuming for the twentieth time the pursuit of an unstable pose until he had given it its essential character, accentuating and concealing at one and the same time the anatomy of the human motor hidden under muslin.

Later, Forain, realist and caricaturist, was in his turn to study that little world, but so as to depict, with mocking laughter, procuresses, dressers, wealthy subscribers to the Opera, — effrontary and vice. Degas, though not ignorant of these, abstained from satire. It is difficult to find in a mere corner of one of his pictures, say against the framework of a flat, a single masculine dress-coat, or, in the very background, the silhouette of a stage-manager or author directing the ballet who is not there by virtue of a sombre value. Everything was geometric, plastic, eurythmic and polychromic in the eyes of our artist. And born of that sagacious discipline was a series of masterpieces. Sometimes they consist of compositions painted in the morning light of dancing-rooms, harmonies in bluish grey and beige, in which an unbound head of hair, a coiffure adorned with flowers, or a coloured « tutu » assumes, in those cold tones, a delectable and powerful value. We experience a faint recollection of Vermeer and Watteau, because of the quiet perfection, the atmosphere of intimacy, and also the supreme distinction of this art, although the painter does not hesitate to emphasize the vulgar ugliness of such or such a face, maring a beautiful body, — the coarse laughter of another, — or a girl who is contorting her body in order to be able to scratch her back. Here the strictly pictorial charm raises everything to the highest level. But in the compositions depicting the entertainment itself, — that ballet which has cost so much labour to bring to perfection, the harmony of golden, pink, blue, turquoise, jade green and purple tones carries away amidst a whirlwind of light and music the recollection of defects, affliction, and banalities. The penetrating artist who knew how to reveal them to us forgot them himself and beheld nothing more than a brilliant transformation, — a miracle issuing from a paltry source, — poesy revealed. Degas felt this so deeply in his impending old age, and when his sight was declining, that it was again to the theme of dancing-girls he returned; he took a delight in transposing them into gigantic flowers, in which colouring took violent precedence over a less sure form, compositions in which we see nothing more save passionate hatchings in pastel, and the corrections, surprises and refinements of a craft so learnedly strange that our thoughts turn to the manner of the last pictures of the nonagenarian Titian as much as to the final lines traced by Hokusaï.

Degas was so anxious to remain exclusively a painter and draughtsman that not only did he avoid laying too great a stress on a satirical intention, which was almost the sole object of Forain in the same domain, he also fought shy of any title such as is given to a « subject » picture; and much were those who drew up catalogues discouraged by the monotony of his titles, which must, nevertheless, be given, though repeated over and over again. The former historical painter thrust aside — perhaps regretfully — the attachment to « subjects » until they became positively distasteful to him. His multitudinous pictures of dancing-girls constitute what may be called the *Modern dancing-girl,* seen under all aspects, surprised in all her attitudes, and above all considered as a theme with plastic variations and, as Verlaine would have said, everything else is literature.

Hence a large number of fragments, each admirable in itself, but which are only detached pieces of what may be called a complete set of armour, or, as you may prefer, the measures of a sonata or symphony. If composition there is, it was not the painter who imagined it, but nature which offered it to him. After his first period, Degas very rarely — only in the case of two or three celebrated pictures produced when he was about forty years of age — made an exception to that rule. Apart from *A Cotton Bureau in New Orleans,* we find *Absinthe* and *The Rape.* The title and appearance of *Absinthe* leads one to conjecture that this picture is intentionally in the vein of a naturalistic novel, with stress laid on café life, moral decay, and the general debasement of a Bohemian through alcohol and the prostitute... As a matter of fact Degas was fascinated by the paradoxical perspective of marble-topped tables which relegate to the background, on the right and almost at the top of the picture, two figures which he « composed » arbitrarily; for the man wearing a bashed-in felt hat was his comrade Marcelin Desboutin, the engraver, with his eternal pipe, and the woman was a friend, the actress Ellen Andrée. Both were to be his models; and though a glass of absinthe is placed before Ellen, it was without any perfidious intention on the part of the painter, who simply had need of an opalescent note at that part of his harmony in grey and black, — an exquisite harmony with all its combination of planes and unexpected arrangement. As to *The Rape,* which has sometimes been given the more discrete title of *An Interior,* there can be no doubt that this masterpiece, one of the most perfect of the XIXth century and comparable to the most beautiful pictures of all time, was conceived, not with any « literary » or merely pictorial intention, but from a profoundly human standpoint.

Was Degas touched by an intimate drama unknown to us? Was his object to depict, as has been suggested, an episode in a novel by his friend Duranty, the sagacious commentator on the work of the early Impressionists? That remains an enigma. In any case, if Degas, against his principles, consented to produce a « subject » picture, he raised it to a high level of generalization, — he, as it were, « serened » it by the perfection of his splendid technique, in which every touch is intentional, whilst revealing a strange tenderness. Amidst the poetic lights and shades of the little bed-chamber of a neat and virginal work-girl, — a room softly lit by a lamp near an embroider's work-basket, and here again how can one help naming Vermeer ? — we find ourselves in the terribly heavy silence which followed on the brutal struggle : a silence broken by the sobbing of the semi-nude victim, bowed down by grief, whilst, with his back to the door, the man, who, now that he has satisfied his lust, is once more correct, but mournfully so, contemplates her despair, though, despite his ennui and remorse, with a glint of madness in his eyes.

There is here that pathetic sobriety, restrained pity, and sadness in the presence of a young girl soiled by the egoistic, epileptic bestiality of a male, which in a singular manner contradicts the legend, if not of the misanthropy, at least of the caustic insensibility that is connected with Degas' name. But all this is suggested by the painter's means. The young girl's bed, the lamp-shade adorned with flowerets, the pink-lined work-box, and the naïve pictures on the wall are so many elements to bring home to us the position and the soul of the little victim, and to these are added her sorry linen corset, torn from her and lying there on the ground, — her slim shoulder caressed by the light. The still-life parts of this picture speak to us the language of her home and form a whole with the tragedy, and without any of these objects having been displaced and arranged towards that end. One can easily imagine how other painters, by a calculated and lascivious disorder, would have emphasized this scene. Degas' infinite tact counselled him to leave everything in its place. One might think that nothing had happened. After a few abominable moments we see nothing more amidst these now peaceful surroundings, save a guilty man and a wretched girl.

These are exceptions which prove the rule. When devoting himself, in series, to the study of women in a state of nudity, Degas abstained, still more than in the case of his *Dancing-girls,* to seek for any other subject or composition than nudity itself, after the manner of the classical painters who considered that to be the supreme object of plastic art. But he could not look upon it and forget his individual tendencies : an almost abstract passion for drawing and the architecture of form, a search for an original setting, a taste for a certain strange and « modern » conception, finally distrust of a too arbitrary form of beauty — that beauty which drew from Baudelaire the remark « that it loathes the movement which distorts the lines ». How could the artist who was insatiable for the surprises of movement not prefer character which opened up so extensive a field of observation? Moreover, along that way he led mediocre and ignorant artists to excesses which in his old age he regarded with scorn, for never in his eyes did character permit of intentional deformation and ugliness.

Finally, his sensitive and stubborn nature, not very pervious to influences, certainly experienced something of the moral pressure of his time, — the pressure of naturalism, which almost ill-naturedly unrobed the woman whom romanticism had over-idealized. From the members of the « corps de ballet », whose defects he had noted, Degas could not pass to the insipid feminine models — disguised as Leda or Biblis — of the painters of the academic school. He sought for them where they were, away from the studio platform, that is to say, in their « cabinets de toilette ». He had too great a love of truth to deny that the nude could only be found there; at any rate nudism in the open air was unknown in his day, and we are far from being invariably delighted with it.

A woman shows herself in a state of nudity only to the man she loves, or to her mirror. Only in the secrecy of the alcove or bath-room is she herself. She is then something entirely different from the dressed-up, painted and adorned creature who appears in public. Degas sought to depict her in her animal-like reality. « I was perhaps wrong », he confessed to a friend at the end of his days, « in considering woman too much as an animal ». A sad confession from a bachelor who had repressed all of man's tenderness, and too late a recognition of the inanity of a scepticism, perhaps due to timidity, and which closed to him the adorable world of love. But the artist was born to give us what he did, and he knew full well what he was capable of doing. That idea of animality contributed to lead the critics and public opinion astray.

They readily believed that Degas was a ferocious misogynist who, with the sledge-hammer of a Huysmans or the substitutes of a Zola, took a delight in belittling woman, in dissecting the dull person she often is, in revealing her defects and little miseries. Such a tendency was not unknown to him, but it did not contaminate his impartial and lucid regard for truth. He observed that fards, corsets, underclothing, and ankle-boots had as slowly deformed the natural and primitive beauty of woman as her occupations or maternity. His models were neither work-girls, nor employees, nor mothers, but prostitutes. He could just as well have noted similar ravages on the bodies of those women of fashion whom his fellow-artists depicted in smart gowns and a garb « à la mode ». Degas was not a searcher after defects; he merely observed and had the courage to record what he saw with his masterly, redoubtable brush. Such audacity, in his day, caused a scandal. It ought not to make him responsible for the horrors which in our day have been exhibited by extremists, who appear to execrate woman up to the point of reducing her to the level of the batrachia. Nevertheless it is true that we owe to Degas the odious harvest of pictures of women in their baths which for thirty years have encumbered our exhibitions, and which show neither his skill, nor his tact, nor his genius. Painters have multiplied to infinity their common place, flat and sometimes basely erotic repetitions of what, in the case of this mathematician of lines and volume, was a human theorem.

Therefore neither love nor its illusions imposed upon his perspicacity, which took account of changes on a woman's epidermis, marks left by corsets and lacing, the vulgarity of her limbs, her drooping breasts. Moreover it has rightly been pointed out that Degas studied woman in the morning, after the hours of night had partially effaced the marks left by her clothing, and when the bath had restored her youth and freshness. So we cannot accuse him of having acted deliberately; and in truth, he many times painted beautiful and fascinating creatures, endowed with young and healthy organisms. But above all, as in the case of dancing-girls, he sought for the various combinations of that plastic figure a nude body is, and whence arms and legs spring; he was attracted by the unexpected nature of their movements, their candid liberty in a place where, screened from all eyes, woman tends and polishes her musculature as though it were a weapon.

Consequently he was led to be more and more daring, up to the point of the oddity of his last big pastels with their jig-saw attitudes, but whose decorative appearance excludes all suspicion of indecent familiarity. These final works mark a return to an almost hieroglyphic conception of form. At the same time that the draughtsman delighted in once more solving new problems of perspective and setting, the colourist revelled in associating flesh-tones in a subdued half-lighting with those of objects, — dressing-gowns, porcelaine, or glass-ware, and became wholly interested in this on account of contrasts and high-lights. He succeeded in a complete coalescence of modelling, value and line, so much so that his figures have the powerful consistancy, the density of bronze, at the same time as being penetrated and haloed by diffused light. And thus « the animal », in its free revels, possesses the same veracious beauty as the horses formerly studied on the turf, whilst anatomical veracity reaches such a pitch of perfection that only a physiologist could perhaps fully appreciate it. This series of nudes, thanks to a triple mastery of mind, eye and hand, possesses a unique value.

Let us say once more : one must search in these works neither for a literary intention, nor a display of misogyny, nor a scabrous tendency. It is true that Degas did not fear to enter dolorous houses of debauch to continue his observations and gaze on nudity in its vulgar and wretched form. But in that line he produced only a few little caricatural monotypes, in an environment where Toulouse-Lautrec, after Forain, was to disport himself so freely and, in the company of prostitutes, avenge his « born diformity » with bravado. Degas was too reserved, too frigid, too enamoured of an abstract and pure art to persist in that direction, at a time when naturalism attached an excessive literary importance to the prostitute, her morals and social rôle, and delighted in hovels, under the belief moreover of finding there, with a sentimentality against the grain, certain grounds for antisocial ranting, which Degas, a conservative bourgeois, held in contempt.

With the same reserve must we consider the few paintings and pastels which he devoted to laundresses and milliners. Once more the key to the man and his art was his passion for truth. He could not satisfy it in what is called society, where everything is artifice, convention, hypocrisy and false modesty; and although he was semi-aristocratic and of refined tastes he never sought for his models there. He found truth — instinctive and acknowledged — among the people, which must not be confounded with the proletariat, compound of wretchedness and hatred. Loathing filthiness and vice, he loved what was natural and sought for its expression in movements demanded by handicrafts, so much so that one may feel astonished he did not seek for them in the fields and manufactories. But he did not believe in the open air and the working man did not attract him. His laundresses — especially the one who stops her work to yawn inordinately in the face of the public — appeared to constitute a challenge to realism.

Here, again, Degas thought solely of professional movement and colour. He studied the exact manner in which the laundress applies her iron, just as he did that of the dancing-girl when she places her foot on the exercising-bar, or that of a woman, squatting in her tub or rising from her bath, when she dries her loins. Pink or yellow dressing-gowns and the bluish-white of starched linen are pretexts for rare and subtle harmonies, whereas, invariably, the attention aroused by the subject leads to the supposition that it is a sort of provocative wager. These pictures are bouquets of tonalities without the least literary flavour. And this also holds good in the case of the few pictures in which the artist satisfied his taste for an unusual, unexpected presentation by depicting the faces of milliners and their customers behind a row of hats seen in the foreground, — a point of view which astonishes no one who has looked through the window into the interior of a milliner's shop; yet this was immediately classed as « things that are not to be done », — in itself a very good reason why an original painter would instinctively attempt to do them. The execution of these hats is delightful, and their capricious intervention in the frame is calculated with a science concealed beneath fancy : it is indeed an example of « wholly reflective » art. Whether it is a question of *Semiramis,* race-course scenes, dancing-girls, or nude women, the subjects change, and the technique; but Degas' method, his vision and manner of synthesizing things seen are invariable.

Yet he cannot have been free from doubts and troubles, and, indeed, this man so averse to confiding in anyone sometimes let slip a few words betraying those regrets, those fears of powerlessness which are common to all really great artists when their efforts are confronted with the infinity of possible realizations. Mediocre, self-satisfied men are in ignorance of these anxieties. But we remain amazed in the presence of Degas' intellectual and plastic constancy, preserved by his jealous isolation and unshakeable independance. In that respect Mallarmé, who loved him, resembled him; both have been incriminated for being odd, defiant and fortuitous, whereas their haughty solitude and profound interior life excluded any concession to the desire to be understood and appreciated. They approached no one, waited serenely for others to come to them, though nobody might ever come.

As regards this, we may say that, bound to all the Impressionists by friendship, Malarmé was not so near to any one of them as he was to Degas, on account of that which was mistaken for singularity.

In the field of engraving, Degas affirmed the same method as is exemplified in his paintings. But perhaps this part of his work, which was long unknown and then inaccurately judged, tells us more of himself than was thought, because, in the case of his canvases, he abstrained from all direct confidences concerning his technique and thought, without advancing quite to the Flaubertian dogma of impersonality. Degas ever devoted himself to engraving, and with a precocious mastery; from the very outset of his career he displayed great curiosity in the technique of this branch of his art, as witness the contrast between two etched portraits executed in Rome in 1857. That of his friend Touruy, a prizeman-engraver of the Villa Médicis, is wholly classical in its treatment, whilst in his own portrait there are delectable liberties not hazarded in his canvases of the same period, — liberties which continued to be affirmed. One may even say that in this field of art the engraver outstripped the painter, gave him counsel and courage despite the scruples inherited from his first period. In black and white, in chiaroscuro were prepared those astounding Rembrandt effects which no one has surpassed; it was there, in little freely-executed works, produced for himself alone and never shown to others, that Degas the painter sought for and found himself : they served him as a gamut and an exercise, side by side with his pictures. Engravings or lithographs, the subjects mattered little, — they were partial replicas of paintings in course of preparation, — sketches made at the « café-concert » or in the « cabinet de toilette », and among them stand out a few marvellous preliminary drawings for a portrait of Manet. What counts is the inventive ingenuity of the methods employed, — the patient researches of a man madly in love with his art, — the determination to extract from matter everything it can give to the one who adores and handles it.

We here take him unaware in the midst of his mania, — to use such a word in its finest acceptation. And this also holds good in the case of his monotypes. He may have found pretexts for these in the green-room of the Opera so as to undertake the projected illustrations for Halévy's *Petites Cardinal,* or in the bath-room, or again, as with some of them, amongst the herd in a brothel; but what holds our attention is the unerringness of the effects and sometimes the latent fantasy of these monotypes, in which all corrections are impossible and chance results that must be foreseen intervene, — results as hazardous as the irregularities that occur when firing porcelain. It would be extremely interesting to be able to follow, at a complete, parallel and accurately dated exhibition, the influence of this part of the artist's production on his paintings, — an influence that gradually freed him from his original classicism without ceasing to bind him to the lesson, and not to the imitation, of the old masters whom this « revolutionary » always, like Manet, venerated.

Finally, there is his sculpture. Degas, like certain other painters, felt a temptation to model, to experiment with more substantial and real volumes than those of painting, which, since it has only two dimensions at its disposal, attains illusion through the play of perspective and values. Here, again, his curiosity for all techniques attracted him, like his tyrannical desire for truth. He sculptured entirely for his own personal satisfaction, in order to test or verify certain daring attitudes before transposing them on his canvases. As exercises and guides, — that was the only importance he attached to these works, but he centred his mind on them with the silent passion he expended in the whole field of plastic art. Sometimes he consulted sculptors, but took little heed of their advice. Lacking knowledge, he sought to invent a technique of his own, and one which responded to the particular objects he had in view. This explains the loss of many statuettes, due to a defective armature; and it also came about that the discontented artist, in a fit of ill-temper, destroyed works he had fashioned with loving care, — to the keen regret of the intimate friends who had admired them. The founder Hébrard published and thus saved seventy-two of these pieces of sculpture, out of very many more, especially dating from 1880, when Degas produced a big figure of a *Fourteen-year-old dancing-girl* in wax.

Degas modelled more and more as his eye-sight declined, and towards the end, when almost stone-blind, he took a dolorous pleasure in kneading modelling-clay or wax with his old, fumbling fingers. This was his last consolation after the period when his infirmity obliged him to paint wholly in broad masses, to take account no longer of line and form, until colour itself faded from his view. When in the presence of his sculptured work, one quickly understands and forgets those imperfections and acts of imprudence which shocked professional sculptors; one remained transfixed with astonishment at Degas' originality, power, and superior gift. Precisely because he had ventured into a field which was not his own, on the fringe of his work as a painter, and, in a way, secretly, he dared to do what would have daunted many a sculptor, in the direction of arabesque and movement, and with an enthusiasm and reflective boldness which creates for him a fellowship with Carpaux and Rodin.

Some of his works, such as *A high-stepping horse, Dismounting from a horse, Dancing-girl examining the sole of her right foot, Dancing-girl : grand arabesque, third motion,* and *Dancing-girl : fourth motion on the left leg,* show by their singular appearance what the artist was aiming at : his desire to reduce animal or human form to an ornamental figure.

His taste for the unforeseen, the fixing of transitory movements, that which is paradoxical yet true, and the not-seen-before was the result of his personal character as much as that of the secret conflict between his early aspirations and the influence of his surroundings and time. After putting his contemporaries off the track, he was reproached by his juniors for that taste, — even by those who borrowed so much from him, sometimes shamelessly and with intentions which he would have reviled. And this great recluse — not at all easy to approach — did nothing to dissipate misunderstandings. Numerous were the painters, critics, and connoisseurs who failed to understand the connection between his works, and who believed in them as disavowals, witnesses to anxieties and contradictions, whereas this almost hermetic art outdistanced the knowledge of the public, which is puzzled by anyone who does not repeat himself.

From what point of view shall we regard him?... Why, from every aspect, and as he was. Whether it is a question of *A Cotton Bureau in New Orleans, The Rape, Absinthe, The Orchestra,* or *The Dancing-class,* — the portraits of Mlle Fiocre, Mlle Dihau, the Duchesse de Montejast and her daughters, Manet, Duranty, or the Duchesse de Morbilli, — *A Race-course Scene, The Star of the Ballet, Laundresses ironing,* or other feminine subjects, we are face to face with that unity in the midst of diversity which makes masterpieces scattered throughout a life-time a concrete whole, — and these masterpieces undoubtedly constitute a mighty contribution to French tradition in art.

Assuredly we are now less interested in the fact that Degas anticipated instantaneous photography, whilst adding that high or deep shadow which the most perfect mechanism cannot give. The recollection of the struggle he had in the heroic days of Impressionism and of the hostility he aroused appears to us in the cold realm of history. We recognize the part in his work which is accidental or due to the influences of a naïve and out-of-date naturalism. Above all must we regret that speculation, after his death, placed an exorbitant price on the slightest sketch of his most scrupulous and so long unrecognized artist, — that, by an irritating abuse, it covered mere fragments with gold, leaving one to judge, when face to face with complete works in exhibitions, of indications to which the author alone held the key. The future will set on one side scraps and stray impulses.

Finally, the relative disfavour shown to Degas by a recent generation (itself already out-of-date) and which speaks ironically of « Monsieur Degas » as it does of « Monsieur Ingres », is of no importance. It is as usual as it is regrettable to see searchers disavow with careless injustice those who preceded them. The services rendered are denied but recognized later. We have not yet reached the time when it will be possible to state exactly Degas' rôle and rank among the great masters of our School. All that we know is that he has had his place marked there, and that his singular and patient genius was sustained by the gifts of one of the most marvellous draughtsmen ever known. With all his methodical audacity he remained a classicist. As to the man himself, one cannot love him; he did not ask to be loved; he was a bitter man, wrapped up in himself as sensitive, almost savage men are. But we cannot refuse him our admiration. No one devoted himself to the worship of art more fervently, — his cult for it was higher than ambition, honours, money, and even friendship. « An artist », wrote Whistler, « at whatever moment he takes a risk, is a monument of solitude which leads to sadness ». And Villiers de l'Isle-Adam said : « Glory is the idea which everyone retains of himself in his own stature ». These two aphorisms sum up Degas in his entirety.

DEGAS IN THE LIGHT OF HIS LETTERS

I N following this study with a selection of letters, thanks to the kindness of the publisher Bernard Grasset, who issued a fine and precious volume of Degas' correspondance, with annotations by M. Marcel Guérin and a preface by M. Daniel Halévy, we have not merely responded to an impulse to give our readers a more complete idea of the artist and of his constant, scrupulous search after methods, so often a subject of conversation with his friends; we have also and above all desired to appeal to Degas himself in order to refute that legend of malignity, misanthropy, and hardness of heart which has been so persistently propagated. This great classical master was unduly considered to be a revolutionary; this man who was so clear minded in the presence of others as he was to himself has been unduly regarded as an ill-natured egoist.

He was aware of this and uttered not a single word of protest. Nay, perhaps he welcomed this judgment, since it served the purpose of keeping intruders from his doorstep. He was sagacious, a master of himself, ironical, sad, and easily offended. From life he expected neither love nor honours; he was wholly possessed by a passion for his art. Was he incapable on that account of affection? Many passages in his letters prove the contrary. He was most simple in his tastes and not over exuberant, though courteous in the old middle-class manner, faithful to anyone who pleased him, and when in a confidential mood he sometimes displayed the ingenuous spontaneity of a child. His guardedness was due to the extreme modesty of his feelings, his hidden caustic humour, and his fear of expecting too much. Long indifferent to political and social life, apart from a few signs of quickly suppressed anger, Degas was a free man, loving painting more than himself, whom he judged without amenity. Severe to others, how much more so was he to himself! Moreover, a hidden anguish obsessed him incessantly and explains many things, — his defective eye-sight and fear of becoming blind. He was almost so when, as M. Daniel Halévy has strikingly said, he resembled ancient Homer, with his poor eyes, snow-white dishevelled beard and hair, wandering tirelessly through the streets of Paris, at the risk of an accident, in order that he might continue to keep in touch with life and movement.

These letters, among which we have only taken the liberty of italicizing certain passages revelatory of the heart of hearts of this man with a mysterious character, possess no epistolary pretention, and the writer certainly never imagined they would one day be published. Nevertheless, instead of setting down his thoughts with brush, pastel, or graver, he sometimes took pleasure in poetical composition. One day he mentioned this to Stephane Mallarmé : « Just imagine I cannot succeed in finishing my sonnet. Yet I have plenty of ideas ». The poet's gentle reply to him was : « My dear Degas, it is not with ideas one makes verses, it is with words ».

In certain of these letters you will find descriptive gifts displayed on the spur of the moment; gaiety, too, and that simple good-nature which the greatest painters possessed from Théodore Rousseau to Corot, Millet, Pissaro, and the days « when one did not get on » to use Degas' own famous retort. The few men who were worthy of the friendship of this recluse knew the full value of these letters and notes, and therefore preserved them piously. Our gratitude is due to them for having assisted us to understand all the better, either thanks to his semi-avowals or through our own cross-checking, the real character of this man who so jealously hid himself in the silence of his studio to contend, in a spirit of profound humility, with his task of attaining perfection.

We are aware of Degas' attachment to a family which caused him a great deal of worry. We also have a knowledge of his profound disdain for money, so little of which he needed to live independently, and it is not without a sense of shame that we witness him mastering his pride when confessing his financial embarrassments and asking for small allowances, thinking the while of the enormous sums which his works, at the close of his life and after death, would bring their owners and the dealers. Finally, we know still better how the keenest sense of the art of observation and of character was able to agree with the temperament, habits, and tastes of a middle-class Parisian classicist, — a paradox that only the intervention of a singular genius can explain.

To Frölich [1].

DE GAS [2] BROTHERS *Undated* (November 27, 1872).
New Orleans.

My dear Frölich,

It was not until today, November 27, that I received your affectionate letters. These most precise Americans read Norwick (Connecticut) instead of what your pen so clearly set down : « Nouvelle-Orléans ». Therefore, through their error your welcome communications have been retarded a fortnight.

The ocean! How expansive it is and how distant I am from you! The « Scotia » on which I came is an English boat, swift and sea-worthy. She brought us (I was with my brother René) in ten to twelve days from Liverpool to New York, the «Empire City».

A wretched crossing! I did not know English, — and I know it hardly better now, — and on English territory, even on the sea, there is a chilliness and conventional distrust which you may already have experienced.

New York, a great city and port. The citizens are very familiar with the great expanse of water; they even speak of the voyage to Europe as the crossing to the other side of the pond. A new people. There is a greater forgetfulness of the English race in America han I ought.

A four days' railway journey at last brought us here. — Take your dear little girl's atlas and look at the distance. Well! (though certainly I do not possess the strength of Thor), I was bigger on my departure than I am now. Air, there is nothing save air here! How many new things I have seen, and how many plans they have suggested to my mind, my dear Frölich! But already I have cast them aside, to think only of my niche and of hollowing it out piously.

Art does not expand, it contracts. And, if you are fond of comparisons at all costs, I would tell you that to produce good fruit one must put oneself in espalier; like a wall-tree one must remain all one's life, with extended arms and open mouth, so as to assimilate that which passes bye and is around one, and live thereon.

Have you read Jean Jacques Rousseau's « Confessions » ? Doubtless you have. You will therefore remember his way of describing his real basis humour when he had retired to the island of the Lac de Saint-Pierre, in Switzerland (it is towards the end of the book), and that he relates that at dawn he went out, wandering this way or that, without knowing whi-

ther; that he examined everything, entered on work which it would have taken ten years to accomplish, and then relinquished it after ten minutes without a regret? Well, I am exactly in that state of mind.

Everything attracts me here. I observe everything. Nay, I will describe everything to you exactly on my return. Nothing pleases me so much as the negresses of every shade, holding little white babies — oh! so white! — in their arms; negresses either in white houses with cinnamon-coloured columns, or in orange-gardens; ladies in muslin in front of their little houses; steamboats with two funnels as high as factory chimneys; fruit dealers with their shops chock-full; and the contrast between the busy, so exactly arranged offices and this immense black animal force, etc., etc. Moreover, the pretty pure-bred women, the charming quadroons, and the well-set negresses!

So I am making plans which would take ten lives to carry out. I shall relinquish them in six weeks, without a regret, to regain and never more leave « my home ».

Dear friend, I thank you a hundred times for your letters and friendship. They give me so much pleasure when I am so far away.

My eyes are a little better. True I am working very little, though at difficult subjects : family portraits, which must be done somewhat to the family taste, with impossible lightings, under disturbed conditions, and with models who, though most affectionate, are somewhat free and easy; models who take you all the less seriously because you are their nephew or cousin.

I have just failed with a large pastel and experience a certain sense of mortification. — If I have the time I count on bringing back something really good, but for myself, for my own room. We must not produce the art of Paris and that of Louisiana indifferently, for that would lead towards the « Monde Illustré ». — Moreover, really it is only a very long sojourn which teaches one the habits of the race; that is to say its charm. — The instantaneous; that is photography and nothing else.

Have you seen that Mr. Schumaker whom you sent to me? He thought that I could easily render him the services he required. He wanted to have himself rubbed with a French hand, as they do at the Turkish baths, immediately after sweating a little. I told him that time was required to sweat out our vices (salutary ones?)

I shall probably be back in January. I shall travel via Havana. But do I understand you to say that you will soon leave us? — Gladly do I wish so if it is on account of your aged mother; for that is a duty. — Well, we shall see a good deal of each other until the Spring. Your little girl will play to me : I crave for music. — Here, this Winter, there is no opera. Yesterday evening I was at the first concert of the year, and a rather poor one it was. A Mme Urto played the violin well, but was accompanied wretchedly. Besides a concert is not an intimate affair, especially here, where they applaud even more stupidly than elsewhere.

1. Lorentz Frölich (1820-1908), a Danish black and white artist and painter, born at Copenhagen. He studied in Munich, Dresden, Rome and, from 1851, in Paris, where he made the acquaintance of Manet in Couture's and Degas' studios. He remained in Paris until 1872, when he returned to Denmark definitely. His drawings illustrating Danish history and poetry, and those he did for children's books give him an honourable position among the best Danish black and white artists.

2. The real family name was written in two words. It was Edgar, the great painter, who was the first to sign his works with the single word : *Degas*. His brothers retained the nobiliary particle, as was their right.

Clotilde must have been delighted to speak her mind on the subject of « Monsieur's » voyage, and doubtless she did not spare her remarks. She is a true maid of the comedy stage, but possesses certain qualities. I threatened not to take her back on my return, and I fear to do so. She is too young for a bachelor and her impudence is really of too strong a flavour. — You must still have your Swedish girl; she appeared to be so attached to you that you will not be able to do without her.

You know only Achille [1], but I believe you have only as yet had a glimpse of him. René [2], my other brother, the last of the three boys, was my travelling companion and even my master. I knew neither English nor the art of travelling in America, so I obeyed him blindly. What stupidities I should have committed without him! He is married, and his wife, our cousin, is blind, almost hopelessly blind, unhappy woman ! She has borne him two children and a third (whose godfather I shall be) is on the way; moreover, as the widow of a young American who was killed in the War of Secession, she brought him a little girl who is nine years of age. — Achille and René are partners. I am writing to you on their office paper. They make a good deal of money and, considering their age, hold a unique position here. — They are liked and held in the highest esteem; a fact of which I am very proud.

Politics! I endeavour to follow a little those of France in the journals of Louisiana. They speak of little else than the supertax on shipping and give M. Thiers expert lessons in Republicanism.

Farewell! Your proverbs are as multitudinous as those of Sancho; possessed of his gaiety you would triple their number. And as a laughter is healthy, I laughed most heartily.

True it is, my dear Frölich, that one feels one has a young head on one's shoulders. That is what David said at Brussels on the eve of his death. Yet it is inevitable to lose something of one's animation, good humour, and sight. You are in a better condition than I am.

You may write to me on the receipt of this; your reply will still find me in Louisiana. — A kiss for your little girl. I clasp your hand and thank you for your friendship.

Greetings to Manet and those near to him. DEGAS.

On re-reading my letter I find that it is indeed frigid compared to yours. Bear me no ill will on that account.

To HENRI ROUART.

DE GAS BROTHERS   New Orleans, December 5, 1872.
New Orleans.

     My dear Rouart,

You will receive this on New Year's day. Wish Mme Rouart a Happy New Year and, also on my be-

half, kiss your children, including the latest addition to your family. Also accept for yourself something you will find in this letter.

I shall certainly be back in January. In order to vary my voyage I count on travelling via Havana. The French transatlantic steamers call there. — I am in a great hurry to meet you again at my place and work there together. One does nothing here, in this atmosphere of cotton. People live for nothing save cotton. The light is so strong that I have not yet been able to do anything on the river. My eyes need so much care that I hardly dare to use them. A few family portraits will be my sole effort; I cannot avoid that, and certainly I should not complain if the work were less difficult, the setting less insipid, and the models less fidgety. Well! this will have been an errand and little else. Manet would see finer things here than I do, but he would not put them to any more use. Our love of art and devotion to it is inspired only by what is familiar; novelty captivates and wearies at one and the same time.

Beautiful and elegant Indian women drawing their green shutters slightly aside, beldames in their ample Madras dressing-gowns on their way to market may be seen in another way than Biard's [3]. But what about afterwards? The orange-gardens and painted houses also appeal to one, as do also the children all in white; and so snow-white when cradled within black arms! But listen! You will remember that, towards the end of his « Confessions », Rousseau, when on the Ile de Saint-Pierre, on the Lac de Brienne, is at last able to meditate entirely at his ease, and how he observes everything indifferently, enters on tasks demanding ten years' work, and then abandons them after ten minutes, without a single regret. That is exactly how I feel. — I observe and admire many things here; I classify their use and the way they can be expressed, mentally. And I shall leave them all without regret. — Life is too short and we possess only a certain requisite amount of strength. Apart from that, long live fine laundering in France!

For the past two days I have been suffering from dysentery and am not a little fatigued. Subnitrate of bismuth will stop that. We have also — hang it! — had a heat in December such as would have satisfied us in June : 24 to 25 degrees at least, in addition to a killing sirocco. A climate which is insupportable in Summer and stupifying in other seasons. One has to be a native, or in the cotton trade; otherwise look out!

A fortnight ago, M. Bujas dined at the house. Naturally we talked about you, and all the nice things that we said surprised no one. The poor man looks very sad and worried, and well he may be! One day I shall go to the ice-factory with him. — You are hardly a better correspondent than I am. Why have you not written me a few lines? When the mail arrives in the morning there is rarely a letter for me and I cannot get used to it.

1. Achille De Gas, Edgar's younger brother, who died in 1893.

2. René De Gas, Edgar's youngest brother, who was born in 1845, and who died in 1920.

3. Is this artist the Biard (François Auguste), a French painter (1799-1882), who travelled a great deal, first of all in the Mediterranean region, then in Lapland and to Spitzberg, and finally in Brazil, where he lived two years?

Behold, my dear friend, my precipitate return home to enter on such a regular life as no one ever led, save Bouguereau, to whose energy and skill I do not dare to aspire [1]. I am seized with a mania for order. — Even a good woman I do not regard as an enemy of this new existence. — And would a few children of my own also be too much? No. — I dream of something well done, a perfect whole (after the manner of Poussin) and the old age of Corot. The very moment has arrived. Otherwise, the old order of life, but less gay, less respectable, *and replete with regret.*

René is in the bosom of his family here and is little given to homesickness. His wife is blind, but superior to her misfortune. They are awaiting a third child, whose godfather I am to be, and who will ignore my everlasting theme. But this is a secret, although the 15th is rent-day speak of it to no one; it is not mentioned to a soul. I do not write about this even to my sister, such being the orders. Papa's wish is that the world should end as though we were not here to put things in order.

The lack of opera is a veritable torture. Poor Estella [2], who is a musician, counted so much upon it. A groundfloor box would have been taken for her, and she would never have missed being there, save at the time of her confinement. In the place of opera we have a company playing comedy, tragedy, vaudeville, etc. — fairly good players and well representative of the talent of Montmartre.

The women here are almost all of them pretty, and to the charms of many of them is added that hint of ugliness without which they would not be perfect. But I fear that their heads are as weak as mine, and two such noddles would be a funny sort of a guarantee for a new household. Alas! I have just let slip a mere nothing, but which may bring me an atrocious reputation. On your honour, Rouart, refrain from ever repeating what I have told you, that the women of New Orleans are weak-minded, refrain from mentioning this to a soul here, or to anyone knowing anyone in these parts, so as to guard against my words being reported here. This is a serious matter. There is no trifling in New Orleans. My death would not wipe out such an affront.

Louisiana must be respected by all her children, of whom I am almost one. — If I told you, after this, that they are good, the insult would be complete, and if repeated this would definitely hand me over to my executioners. I am joking a little. There is something captivating about Creole women. A short time ago I spoke about Rousseau, whom, as I am reading him again in the evening, I readily quote.

Julie made herself loved because she appeared ready to be loved (read once more a letter from Claire to her friend); there is the tenderness of the 18th century in their air. Many belonging to those families

came here in short skirts and that perfume has not yet evaporated.

Farewell! My desire was to fill these four pages and give you pleasure at my own sweet will. If I have failed in this, punish me in the same manner. Moreover, I am in the office of De Gas Brothers, where one can write fairly well. De Gas Brothers are held in high esteem here and I am rather flattered to note it. They will amass a respectable fortune.

In conclusion, let me repeat my best wishes to Mme Rouart for a Happy New Year, together with kisses for your children and an affectionate handshake for yourself.

Your devoted friend

DEGAS.

To HENRI ROUART.

Paris, August 8 (1873).

My dear Friend,

You cannot do better than sing the praises of the country. If your singular correspondent has not quite burnt down the Opera [3], he has at least rented two rooms... at Croissy. When he has fairly well assured himself of his repose he will go there and, exactly like a third-rate actor, take his nature cure. He is thinking of going on foot to Rouen, following the banks of the Seine, and, now and then, stepping aboard a barge, or taking the railway when he comes across it. Therefore, with a stick in my hand, but without a parasol, I can feel myself studying tones and the curve of the road as it winds amidst little hills, and especially in the evening, the hour for soup and a sound snooze in sheets more or less white. Ah! the redolence of cooking and a bottle of Roche-Guyon : there you have my motto. *It is nature's motto.* But I expect from it much less happiness than you do, — only a little good for my eyes and a little relaxation for the remainder of me.

.   .   .   .

The completion of my pictures, pastels, etc., is never ending... How long it takes and how my last good years slip bye under conditions of mediocrity! Very often I sorrow over my poor life. Yesterday I attended the funeral of Tillot's [4] father. Lippmann told me the other day that you would soon return and I had a gleam of hope of finding you there. In order to lessen somewhat the force of your reproaches I am writing to you. My letter will perhaps be sent back from Portrieux to Paris, but it will reach you and perhaps

---

1. Is this a sincere or ironical tribute? In any case, Degas and his friends spoke of a painting with too much finicky detail as « Bougereauté ».

2. Mme René De Gas, née Musson.

3. An allusion to the burning of the Opera-house of the Rue Le Peletier, in 1873.

4. Charles Tillot, a painter, the friend of Degas and the Rouart Brothers, and who exhibited with the Impressionists. For a long time he inhabited Barbizon, where he became intimate with Théodore Rousseau and J. F. Millet. He nursed Millet during his last illness with great devotion. Tillot had a sound taste for art. He was a collector of Oriental works of art, Japanese prints, and other artistic treasures of the Far-East. His Parisian studio was at 42, Rue Fontaine-Saint-Georges. An exhibition of his works was held in April, 1895, at the Durand-Ruel Gallery.

will appease you. The heart is like many instruments : one must rub it and often use it, if it is to retain its polish and work well. As to my heart, you are still the polisher, rather than its owner.

To Faure [1].

Undated (1876).
Friday.

My dear Faure,

You told me that you intended, at the end of this week, to complete your payments to me for the picture, although it is not yet finished. This is too soon : I have no need of the money yet.

But if you can let me have by tomorrow another 500 francs you will greatly oblige me. I will finish paying everything I promised last Saturday.

You are singing, I believe, this evening. Do not forget to remind Mérante [2] of the photographs he promised me yesterday. I am anxious to see them and combine what I can do with the gift of this dancer.

So long!

Degas.

To Faure.

Undated (1876).

My dear Faure,

I am going to deliver « Robert le Diable » [3] on Saturday and « Les Courses » [4] on Tuesday.

I have had to earn my wretched living so as to be able to occupy myself a little on your behalf; despite my daily fear of your return, I had to turn out little pastels. Excuse me if you can still do so.

Moreover this has been very bad weather for my eyes.

Yours truly

E. Degas.

To Faure.

Undated. The postage-stamp on the envelope bears the date : March 1877.

Wednesday.

My dear Monsieur Faure,

It was with great sadness that I received your letter. I prefer to write to you rather than see you.

Your pictures would have been finished a long time

ago if I had not been daily under the necessity of earning money. You cannot imagine with what a multitude of worries I am overwhelmed [5].

To morrow is the 15th and I am going to pay something, and until the end of the month I shall have a little spare time. I am going to devote this fortnight almost entirely to you. Once more have the kindness to wait until then.

Yours truly

Degas.

To Bracquemond.

Undated (1880).

My dear Bracquemond,

It opens on the 1st of April. The posters will be up tomorrow, or on Monday, with bright red letters on a green ground. There has been a big tussle with Caillebotte as to whether the names shall be there or not. I had to give way to him and let them appear. When will this printing of people's names so that they stand out cease ?

Both Mlle Cassatt and Mme Morisot were absolutely against appearing on these posters. Yet last year's plan was followed, and Mme Bracquemond's name is not there — which is idiotic. All sound reasons and taste were powerless against Caillebotte's stubbornness and the inertia of the others.

In consequence of the unrestrained publicity of Nittis [6] and Monet (in the « Vie Moderne »), our Vth exhibition [7] ought to be your glory. Next year, upon my word, I will so arrange things as to prevent this continuing. I am grieved and humiliated.

Start to bring your exhibits. Probably two panel-screens will be arranged : one in the middle of the room with four windows and the other in the entrance hall. You can display on them your entire stock of engravings [8].

So long!

Degas.

If you insist upon it and Mme Bracquemond is of the same opinion, her name will be printed on the second thousand posters during the Exhibition. Please reply.

---

1. The celebrated singer of the Opéra, and a great collector of pictures by the Impressionists.

2. A dancer who became a dancing-master of the ballet at the Opéra.

3. The « Nuns » Ballet in *Robert the Devil*, now in the Ionides collection at the South Kensington Museum.

4. Probably the large picture *At the Races,* in which gentlemen riders are depicted near a victoria in which a lady is seated (No. 166 of the Camondo collection in the Louvre).

5. Degas doubtless alludes to the family burdens he had accepted and which were a heavy load on his shoulders for many years.

6. Nittis (Joseph de) (1845-1884), painter and engraver, born at Barletta (Italy).

7. The Vth Exhibition of paintings (the Vth Impressionist exhibition) was held from the 1st to the 30th of April, 1880, at 10, Rue des Pyramides, at the corner of the Rue Saint-Honoré.

8. Bracquemond exhibited his « etchings for the ornamentation of services of faïence and porcelain »; the series of etchings of animals and flowers for the celebrated service in faïence with a blue border (known as the Bracquemond service) of the Maison Rousseau, Rue Coquillière, Paris.

To CAMILLE PISSARRO.

Undated (1880).

My dear Pissarro,

I congratulate you on your ardour. I hastened to Mlle Cassatt's with your parcel. She pays you the same compliments as I do on this subject.

Here are the proofs. The general blackish or rather greyish tint arises from the zinc, which in itself is greasy and retains the printer's ink; and the plate is not sufficiently planished. I can well imagine that at Pontoise you are not as well placed as regards that point as in the Rue de la Huchette [1]. All the same you must have something smoother.

However, you can see what resources the process has. You must also practice the laying of grains, so as to obtain, for example, a sky with a uniform and fine grey. That is very difficult if Maître Bracquemond is to be believed. But when your desire is to produce original art engravings, it is perhaps fairly easy.

Here is the method. Take a very smooth plate, — an essential, you must understand. Rid it of every trace of grease with whitening. Beforehand you have dissolved resin in very pure alcohol. When this solvent is poured on to the plate, after the manner employed by photographers when they pour collodion on to their glass (and take care, as they do, to let all the superfluous liquid pour off) [2], it evaporates and leaves the plate covered with a more or less thick layer of resin in the form of minute particles. When biting the plate you obtain a more or less dark *semis* according to whether it is a short or long biting. To get flat tones that is necessary; but when less regular effects are wanted you can obtain them with a stump, or the finger, or any other pressure on the paper covering the soft ground. Your soft ground appears to me to be a little too fat; you have used a little too much fat or suet.

And after this did you blacken your ground, so as to obtain that brownish tone behind the picture? That is a very pretty effect. Try something larger on a better plate. As regards colour. I will print the next plate you send me in a coloured ink [3]. I have also other ideas for the colour plates. Also try something more *finished*. It would be delightful to see the contour of the cabbages well-defined [4]. Remember that you must make your début with one or two fine plates.

In a few days' time I shall set to work myself.

I am told that Caillebotte is painting from his windows a picture entitled « Des refuges du Boulevard Haussmann » (Street-islands on the Boulevard Haussmann).

Can you find anyone at Pontoise who is able to cut out of very thin copper things traced by you? This sort of patterns might be placed on a line or soft ground etching, and by means of porous wood blocks saturated with water-colour the uncovered parts printed. Some pretty trial prints in colour, original and curious, might thus be produced. Work on that a little if you are able. I will shortly send you some experiments of my own in that direction [5]. It would be economical and a novelty. That would do for us, I believe, to begin with.

There is no need to compliment you on the artistic quality of your vegetable-gardens. Only, as soon as you feel you are a little more used to things, try something bigger and more complete.

Be of good heart! DEGAS.

To HENRI ROUART.

Paris, Tuesday, October 26.

My dear Rouart,

Thank you for your letter in pencil. It appears that the sirocco dries up ink, just as it does oil-colours and the vigour of painters.

Ah! how deeply I regret that I was unable to accompany you down there and see those good friends. Moreover, — and to tell you this immediately is a rare thing for me to do, — I am in the humour for appreciating something of Nature on a grand scale. You would have had a metamorphosized companion and one with the strength to vibrate exactly like another. A few big drawings or pastels would perhaps have been produced by a frantic Grévin. And the sublime would certainly have done me as much good as it would a wise man.

We can hardly see here : in the afternoon especially we are in darkness. I should like to finish the Ephrusi picture [6], and although the canvas and the drawings are ready it hardly advances at all. Yet at the end there is good money, — impatiently awaited.

Bring me back some fine features, such as you depict. Have you taken pastels with you? Water-colour is weak [7]... nevertheless Delacroix!

At Burty's there is a tiger by him in pastel which, under glass, look like a water-colour. It is drawn in pastel, very lightly applied on a somewhat smooth paper. It throbs with life, and the means to this end are fine. I am going to write to Cherfils [8]. I have

1. Where the planisher Godard had his place of business.

2. Here the writer made a little sketch of a plate held in a hand, with the drops falling from it.

3. We do not know exactly to which plates reference is here made, but Degas himself printed or had printed, in his presence, artist's proofs in red, reddish brown, burnt Sienna, Vandyck brown and even Prussian blue of the plate entitled « Crépuscule avec meules » (Haystacks in the Twilight). See No 23, in Delteil's catalogue.

4. Pissarro produced a soft ground etching representing a « Champ de choux » (A field of cabbages). See No. 29, in Delteil's catalogue.

5. As far as we are aware, Degas never carried out these experiments. The process of making prints with wood-blocks and water-colour was practised by Gaugain, who engraved direct on to the wood.

6. Charles Ephrussi, owner and editor of the «Gazette des Beaux-Arts ».

7. Degas rarely used water-colour.

8. Alphonse Cherfils, the friend of P. Lafond, the former curator of the Pau Museum, and of Degas. Degas painted on a panel, with turpentine, a study depicting his two friends Cherfils and Lafond examining a canvas (in the Marcel Guérin collection). This study was reproduced in colours as a frontispiece to the second volume of P. Lafond's book on Degas (published by Floury).

neglected him too much. Yet it is not often that we meet people so affectionate, so intelligent as he is.

The Cassatts have returned from Marly. Mlle Cassatt has taken possession of a groundfloor studio which appears to me to be not very healthy. What she has done in the country looks very good in the studio light; it is much stronger and has more nobility than what she did last year. So long! We shall chat more at our ease in the Rue de Lisbonne when in front of your articles [1]. I write to you in fear of your malediction.

I am setting off for the Boulevard Voltaire to dine at your brother's house. On all sides there is nothing but mud, mud... and umbrellas. Nevertheless the hours of evening are indeed beautiful.

To ALEXIS ROUART.   *Undated* (1882).

My dear Friend,

This little trial carbon-pencil [2] print I made only yesterday. You see what a pretty grey effect it gives. Pencils made of emery are requisite [3]. Give me an idea so that I can make them myself. On Friday I was unable to talk about this with your brother. Thanks for the stone you have sent me. It scratches the copper delightfully. Is it a conglomerate such as Denis Poulot makes? With a magnifying glass I read the name Delanoue aîné.

On what can I use it as an etching-needle?

No time to make really serious experiments. There are always articles to be turned out. The last one is a tint-drawing on a fan for M. Beugniet [4]. All my thoughts are concentrated on engraving, yet I attain nothing.

Kindest regards   DEGAS.

To HENRI ROUART.   May 2 (1882).

. . . .

Lafond has written me a few words He is coming here soon to see his charcoal in the Salon, but will leave

immediately for his Lycee at Pau. The fine weather is here again and doubtless returns to you also? Sunday — the great varnishing day. There is an astounding Whistler, most refined but of such a quality!

Chavannes — noble and somewhat re-hashed — makes the mistake of displaying himself impeccably dressed and full of pride in a large portrait which Bonnat [5] has done of him, with a big dedication on the gravel, on which he and a massive table, with a glass of water on it, *pose* (Gorcourt style). Manet — simple and subtle — a blank playing-card — a piece of Spanish bluff — a painter.... Well, you will see for yourself! Poor Bartholomé is skyed and naively demands that his two exhibits be given back to him.

To BARTHOLOMÉ.

Paris, August 5, 1882.

My dear Friend,

I surprised you. Quite true! I succumb, but recover again very quickly. I arrived on Monday evening and found your note, and on Tuesday morning, Rue Bayard, they told me that you had already decamped the evening before. Eight days at Etretat was a great deal for me. Halévy is a good sort, but funereal [6]. I do not know how to play either piquet or billiards, nor how to curry favour with people; nor to be even agreeable in society. I believe I rather bored them and that they came to the conclusion I am lacking in resource.

. . . .

When do you return? For I am alone here. Paris is charming; and is not work the finest thing when one is in the vein?

Monday morning, — a sitting with Pagans [7] before he leaves for Spain. Mme Camus [8] is said to have cried, one day, with vexation and passion for the guitar in the presence of a good-hearted general who was giving her lessons on it.

5. This portrait of Puvis de Chavannes was painted by Bonnat in exchange for the fresco which Puvis de Chavannes did for Bonnat's house in the Rue de Bassano. It was exhibited at the Salon of 1882.

6. At that time Ludovic Halévy was bowed down through mourning and worry, which caused him to give up writing for the stage.

7. Pagans, a Spanish singer and guitarist, much liked by M. Degas *père*. Degas painted several portraits of him, singing and accompanying himself on the guitar, whilst M. Degas *père* sat by his side, listening to him in a state of deep meditation. One of these portraits is reproduced in the first volume of P. Lafond's book on Degas (Floury, Paris). The other was exhibited at the Degas exhibition at the Georges Petit Gallery in 1924 (No. 8); and at the Henri Fèvre sale, in June 1925, was sold for 85,000 francs.

8. Mme Camus, wife of one of Degas' friends. He painted a magnificent portrait of her, seated at the piano. It was exhibited at the Salon of 1869. Sold at the first sale of Degas' pictures, in May 1918, under No. III, it is now in the Alphonse Kann collection, at Saint-Germain-en-Laye. It was on view at the Degas exhibition in 1924, under No. 34, and more recently at an exhibition of masterpieces of the XIXth century, at the Rosenberg Gallery. At the sale of the contents of Degas' studio there were numerous studies in pencil and pastel for this portrait.

1. By the word « articles » Degas designated pictorial works in general; his own as well as those of others. See his next letter.

2. The carbon-pencil of an arc-lamp, called an electric pencil. Several of Degas' etchings were engraved by this means : notably the little « Ellen Andrée » (No. 20 in Loys Delteil's catalogue), the « Danseuses entre les portants » (Dancing-girls behind the framework of a flat) (No. 23, L.D.), the two etchings : « Miss Cassatt au Louvre » (No. 29-30, L.D.), the « Petit cabinet de toilette » (No. 34, L.D.), and especially « Sortie du bain » (No. 39, L.D.) which is very probably the work mentioned in this letter. It was an etching engraved at Alexis Rouart's, Boulevard Voltaire.

One evening, when Degas was dining with his friend, a hard glazed frost prevented him returning home, so he passed the night at Rouart's. On waking up in the morning he asked for a copper-plate saying : « I have a desire to do an etching ». A copper-plate was found in Alexis Rouart's workshop, and upon it, by means of the carbon-pencil of an arc-lamp, Degas engraved the first state of the « Sortie du bain ». This anecdote was related by Alexis Rouart himself.

3. These carbon-pencils are a conglomerate of powdered emery.

4. A picture-dealer of the Rue Laffitte.

X... sent me a strong article from the « Standard », in which, in the course of a few courteous and affected lines, I am caressed. I would pinch it likewise if I were not afraid of pricking the abscess before it is ripe. I ought to have tried to catch Gervex, a new-comer, decorated, and more useful.

To Bartholomé.
Undated (1883, the year of Manet's death).
Wednesday.

A change of air, even in this wretched weather, would surely do good. It would cure one of being heated all the day by a stove, and also heated by the work of painting. I must force myself, now that the days are getting long, to remain in the studio only half a day, morning or afternoon, and walk about. *Ambulare* [1] — there's a new motto! — *postea labore*.

Manet is lost [2]. That Dr. Hureau de Villeneuve is said to have poisoned him with spurred rye. A few newspapers have, it is said, already taken care to announce his approaching end. They have, I hope, read them at his home, in his presence. He has no inkling of his condition, gangrene in one foot.

To Henri Rouart.
October 16 (1883).

My dear Friend,

This letter will just reach you in Venice... We enterred Alfred Niaudet [3] on Saturday. Do you remember the evening with guitars at home, almost a year and a half ago? I counted those present and we were twenty-seven. Four of them have now departed. Mlles Cassatt were to have come, and one of them is now dead. That would have made a fifth. *Let us stick like glue to this coil, wholly Republicain though it may be.*

. . . .

You love nature as much as you do humidity. All the same give me the pleasure of leaving your two friends momentarily in order to enter, dry-shod, the Labia Palace, to see, half for me and half for you, the frescoes of Tiepolo. Forain, yes, Forain, gave me yesterday evening, on a table of the Café Larochefoucauld, a general survey of them, and he concluded by comparing them to a poster by Chéret. That is his manner of expressing admiration. It is perhaps no worse than any other.

. . . .

Had I accompanied you I should have started on my portrait of your daughter, in the midst of Venice, where her hair and complexion were formerly celebrated. But I had to remain here because there are quarter-days.

1. It is curious to note that from this period Degas became fascinated with the idea of those walks which afterwards became a veritable perambulatory mania. Towards the close of his life he walked for hours on end in Paris, without an object in view. He was then already almost blind and incessantly ran the risk of being crushed to death.
2. Manet died in the Spring of 1883.
3. Alfred Niaudet, a cousin of Mme Ludovic Halévy, and who died in October 1883. Degas painted his portrait, which, under No. 61, was on view at the Degas exhibition in 1924.

To Henry Lerolle [4].
December 4, 1883.

My dear Lerolle,

Hurry up and go to the Alcazar, Rue du Faubourg-Poissonnière, to hear Thérèsa.

It is near the Conservatoire, and it is better. Already and long ago it was said, I know not who the man of taste was who said it, that one must apply oneself to Gluck. You are all steeped in Gluck at the present time [5]. The time has come to go and hear that admirable *artiste*.

She opens her great mouth and there issues forth the most rudely, most delicately, most spiritually tender voice imaginable. And as to soul and taste, where could one find them more elevated? It is admirable.

Anyway, on Thursday at the house of *my* musician.
With kindest regards   Degas.

To M. and Mme Bartholomé.
Undated.

Monsieur Degas, deeply moved, presents his New Year greetings to Monsieur and Madame Bartholomé. He is also obliged to confess that he does not possess a visiting-card and that, when he finds people are not at home, he writes his name on the margin of the concierge's newspaper ; or an envelope is handed to him. Other people's delicacy as regards friendship gives him infinite delight. May the others continue!

To Mme Bartholomé (née de Fleury) [6].
Undated.

Dear Madam,

Deign to grant me yet another little holiday on Wednesday. Something surprising has happened. A painter, Henry Lerolle [7], who, I am told, is making good progress towards being decorated, in the free interval between the Salon and the Triennial or National Exhibition, and who I knew possesses a certain fortune, has just invited me to dinner. His right to do this is of recent date, but it is fairly wide in its scope. Acting in concert with his wife, who is reputed to be his guide, he has just, under her influence, purchased from Durand-Ruel [8] a little picture of horses by me.

And so he writes to me to express his admiration (in Saint-Simon style), saying that he wishes to feast

4. Letter quoted by Mme Jeanne Raunay in « Souvenirs anecdotiques sur Degas » (*Revue de France,* March 15, 1931).
5. At the house of the composer Ernest Chausson, brother-in-law of Henri Lerolle, musicial recitals of « Orphée », in which Degas took great pleasure, were being given.
6. Bartholomé's first wife.
7. Concerning the painter Lerolle and his Salon, see Maurice Denis' article in the *Revue de Paris,* for November 10, 1930.
8. This picture was purchased in 1864 by the painter Lerolle from Durand-Ruel, in whose window, in the Rue de la Paix, it was exhibited for the sum of 2,500 francs; a high price in those days. It was reproduced in the second volume of P. Lafond's book on Degas (Floury, Paris), and also in the catalogue (No. 45) of the 1924 Degas exhibition, at the Georges Petit Gallery. It now belongs to the heirs of M. Henry Lerolle.

me in the company of his friends; and although most of the legs of the horses of his good picture (mine) are badly placed, I have a good mind, modest though I am, to let myself be held in esteem a little at table. For once only, dear Madam, let me intoxicate myself, on the other side of the water, behind the Invalides, with the perfumes of glory. If nothing, even the wine, succeeds in making me drunk, why should I not, having taken a breath of air, appear before you for a few moments about half past ten p.m.?

Your friend   DEGAS.
Monday.

TO BARTHOLOMÉ.

August 16 (1884).

My dear Friend,

Are you going to levy a distress? What will you seize in the horrible human heart? I know not where my friends will be able to sit down, for there are no more chairs. There is the bed, which cannot be seized, and on which I slumber really too long, for this morning, at seven o' clock, after having momentarily left it to open the window and write to you before the postman went bye, I remained between the sheets so as to enjoy the morning more comfortably. Yes, I am becoming ungrateful, and I am becoming so in a comatose state, which makes this ill without a remedy. Having cut art in two, as you remind me, I am about to cut off my own head, and Sabine [1] will preserve it as a matter of form in a wide-mouthed bottle.

Is it the country, or the burden of my fifty years which makes me feel so heavy, so disgusted as I am? People find me full of gaiety because I smile so stupidly and in so resigned a manner. I am reading « Don Quixote ». Ah! happy man and what a noble death was his.

May your wife, in splendid health as she is, curse me not over much and ask if I'm worth the trouble. Let her reserve her anger and tenderness for a man who is young, confident, proud, simple, bold and soft, supple and hard, a painter and writer, a writer and father. And, still more astonishing than he may think, let him write or have written, or exclaim : Long live J. F. Raffaëlli. Believe me he is still the man we need.

Your medal ought to fill me with indignation. But I welcome it as though it were of gold. Long live Sandoval also, the tenancy man, the man who pays his rent. I am cracking heavy jokes with you, and much against my inclination.

Ah! what has become of the days when I felt myself strong, logical, and full of plans! I am rolling down the hill very rapidly, I know not whither, and wrapped up, as though in packing-paper, in a multitude of wretched pastels.

Au revoir! And with the most sincere expressions of friendship towards your excellent wife and yourself.

DEGAS.

---

1. Sabine Neyt, one of Degas' servants, and who died at his house in the Rue Pigalle.

TO HENRY LEROLLE [2].

August 21, 1882.

My dear Lerolle,

If you reply to me you will certainly say that I am a strange fellow. Why I did not write to you before your departure and the receipt of the box of sugared almonds [3] I cannot really say.

If you were a bachelor and fifty years of age (a month ago), you would have those moments when you shut yourself up like a door, and not only against your friends. I suppress everything in my immediate surroundings and when at last alone I annihilate, nay, immolate myself through sheer disgust. I have formed too many plans and consequently find myself blocked and powerless. I have lost the thread of my ideas. I thought that I should always have enough time; what I failed to do, what I was prevented doing, in the midst of my worries and despite my infirmity of sight, I never despaired of beginning some fine morning.

I crammed all my plans into a cupboard, the key of which I always carried about with me, and I have lost that key! In short, I feel that I cannot rid myself of the comatose state in which I am. I keep myself busy, as people who do nothing say, and that is all.

I write all this under no great stress; to have asked you humbly to pardon me for my rudeness would have sufficed. But I recollect that Alexis Rouart told me that you are going, on leaving Paris; to somewhere near Vimoutiers.

This letter, addressed to 20, Avenue Duquesne, will follow you and this time (it is you who have to reply to me) I am sure of the reply.

I must add that I am also near Vimoutiers, at the house of a friend of my childhood [4], and perhaps only a few leagues from you. Write to me at the Château de Ménil Hubert, via Gracé (Orne).

I will come and see you immediately if you are where I believe you are.

My kindly recollections to your wife.

Yours very truly   D.

TO DURAND-RUEL [5].

Undated.

Dear Sir,

My servant will call upon you for a little money. This morning I received from her a threat that a dis-

---

2. Letter quoted by Mme Jeanne Raunay (loc. cit.).

3. Sugared almonds distributed on the occasion of the baptism of one of Henry Lerolle's sons.

4. Paul Valpinçon, the son of Edouard Valpinçon, the friend of Ingres, and father of Mme J. Fourchy, had been Degas college chum and remained one of his most devoted friends. Degas painted several portraits of him, one being in the Marcel Guérin collection. He it was whom Degas painted with a light-coloured beard and a top-hat, sitting on the box-seat of a barouche depicted in the picture of the Durand-Ruel collection entitled « Calèche aux courses » (A barouche at the races).

5. MM. Durand-Ruel possess a very large number of letters similar to this one. All are requests for money. Durand-Ruel was Degas' banker and made advances of money, which the artist repaid in the form of works.

tress will be levied on me for taxes, of which I have paid more than half. It appears that the State demands the balance. Fifty francs will suffice. But if you can give her a hundred she will retain something for herself. I left her with very little, and I am prolonging my stay here for a short time, since the weather is so fine.

Ah! I am going to stuff you with my goods this Winter and you will stuff me with your money.

It is most annoying and humiliating to have to run after a five franc piece as I am doing.

A thousand thanks.

DEGAS.

Wednesday.   Château de Ménil Hubert, near Gracé (Orne).

To DURAND-RUEL.

Undated.

Dear Monsieur Durand-Ruel,

I have safely received and cashed your money-order. If you can send me another fifty francs I shall be provided for. I count on being back by Wednesday evening. Enough of this dawdling!

You are right. What a beautiful country. Every day we are making excursions in the neighbourhood and these would end by turning me into a landscape-painter if my wretched eyes did not refuse to agree to such a transformation.

I am very sorry for you in your prison-like Paris. And yet you will see with what serenity I am going to return there.

Friendly greetings.

DEGAS.

Saturday.   Still at Halévy's, Rue de la Grève, Dieppe.

To HENRI ROUART.

Undated.
Monday morning.

My dear Friend,

I knew that you were going to return soon and that I could not write to you. Moreover, I had so little to tell you. Besides, one often writes to one's friends to say nothing, and yet that means one is so pleased to receive a few lines from them, to know that they are thinking of you, and are your friends.

So first of all, therefore, present my compliments to Mme Rouart. The waters did her good last year. Most probably she will benefit by them this year still more. And that is already something.

X... has probably replied to you. That guide of the Pyrenees gave me the impression the other day that he was very depressed. We met in the neighbourhood of the Maison Goupil, and he appeared to be fairly well convinced that the cash department of that great firm was closed to him for ever. He was inclined to think or wanted to assure me that Cabanel had something to do with it, if I had not told him that this was another illusion and that all this came from higher and more distant quarters.

I am joking, my dear friend, for want of something better to do. How can one listen seriously to other people's misfortunes when, as regards that, one feels oneself to be so far more burdened than they are? Really enough of this! so many necessary things, altogether, do I lack. Above all my sight (health is the most precious of all possessions) is not at all what it ought to be. You will remember that one day, when speaking to me about someone who was growing old, you said « that he could not put things together », a medical expression used in the case of those who are mentally impotent. That expression I have not forgotten. Well, my eyes can no longer « put things together », or with such difficulty that I am often tempted to give it up and continue to slumber.

It is also true that the weather is most variable. As soon as it is dry and bright I can see very much better, although some time must elapse before I get used to the strong light which hurts me in spite of my smoked glasses. But soon there is a return of dampness and I find myself as I am now : my eyes burnt up yesterday are stewed to a jelly to-day. When and how will this end?

To BARTHOLOMÉ.

Undated. Friday.
(December 19, 1884).

. . . .

I awaited your news instead of hastening towards them. The truth is that I have not much heart. And what I did possess has not been increased by family and other worries. These left me with only what they could not take away, very little, enough for me, but hardly sufficient for my good friends.

You two have ever been — and so promptly — full of kindness and kind actions towards me. Both of you are now, one ill, the other in the midst of trouble and uncertainty, and I chose such a time not to return what you gave me! Such is the action of a man who would end and die in solitude, without any happiness whatsoever.

To BARTHOLOMÉ.

Undated.

It is there and I have once more gazed upon it this morning, *with its red loins full of creases.* So thinks and writes Goncourt when his friend Bartholomé sends him a pumpkin.

We shall eat it for supper on Sunday, my dear friend, myself and a few people connected with the Opera who know how to eat. I will strive not to eat more than they do, even less.

When are you returning? I ask you that, forgetting that you love the fields, that you are a lover of gardens, and that if there I shall one day come to you and deposit a Wagnerian paving-stone on your head. I am, then, a bear, in slight degree a ruler over modern plastic art, but more usually a taster of the honey from Mount Hymettus of the Opera « Sigurd ».

I have seen this « Sigurd » one more, but missed meeting Reyer again at the Brasserie Muller, on the right of the monument. — Speaking to the divine

Mme Caron [1] I compared her to the figures of Puvis de Chavannes, who she did not know. Rythme, rythme, may your excellent wife bring it back to me one day soon, facing the infamous Reyer, the ruler of this score!

This pumpkin was energetically designed, was it not? Ah! if only one could draw a noble bust with round shoulders like that. In default of big people who will not allow themselves to be seen (Sabine), there are children built on these lines.

I have written a few lines to your sister-in-law. Renew my compliments to her. Most friendly greetings to both of you. You can write to me. Apart from vegetables, a letter gives me pleasure.

Best wishes.

DEGAS.

Wednesday : news?

To BARTHOLOMÉ.

Naples, January 17 (1886).

My dear Friend,

Today, Saturday, I was to have gone to Pouzzales, on Lake Fusaro, to Baia, and other places, bent on a tour to see what I had never seen before during all my journeys to Naples.

It is raining and I am writing, which is not a particularly painful operation since I am writing to you. Recognizing my writing, your wife will once more not fail to open this letter, whilst you are on those errands you carry out so well. Soon we shall meet again, for it will not be long before I return. I do not feel myself capable of transacting such a piece of business as this, and my pushing on to here was only a mere owner's pilgrimage. You found my letter very sad and you are not far wrong. With me interest and sentiment are singularly in opposition, and on those two points I can defend myself very badly. I have also a horrible fear of advocates and solicitors. But through whose agency can I arrive at estimates?

I am copying and translating many deeds and contracts, many documents; and I shall arrive with all these papers in Paris, to fall into the arms of a Rouart, or any other friend well up in the questions interesting me. In the Spring I shall return to Naples better armed. That seems to me to be the best thing to do. All I have lost is a month which might have been less arduous.

I am not forgotten in Paris : you are not the only one, my dear friend, who writes to me. But no one writes better than you do, or more affectionately, not even the women. Young Jacques [2] has got himself introduced to Mme Howland and his stock of tittle-tattle will gain thereby. *Nihil humanum* must be insupportable to support. I *speak of former times, for, apart from the heart, it seems to me that everything*

in me is growing old proportionally. And there is even something artificial in this heart. The dancing-girls have sewn it up in a pink silk bag, and the pink silk is somewhat faded, like their dancing-sandals.

I am curious to see your picture. How pretty is the photograph of the drawing you have given me! *But one must do the same subject over and over again, ten times, nay a hundred. Nothing in art should resemble an accident, not even movement.*

To BARTHOLOMÉ.

CONTINENTAL HOTEL   Tangiers
Tangiers (Morocco)   Wednesday, September 18 (1889).

My dear Bartholomé,

I cannot do less than write to you from such a place. Can you imagine me on the back of a mule, forming part of a cavalcade which a guide, in a violet silk gown, is leading, on the sandy sea-shore, and along dusty country roads, around and then through Tangiers? Can we, another year, make once more the journey which, to my sorrow, you are making very nearly alone ? The guide in the silk gown knows French, but not as you speak it.

We love in nature the men who were not unworthy to come into contact with her. I tell you this because Delacroix passed this way. The boat brought us here in grey weather, but there was to be seen in it much more of the greyness of pearls than that of slate.

I have nothing to tell you; I write just to date my friendship for you from Tangiers. In a week at the most I shall be in the Rue de Chaillot. Tomorrow, return to Cadix, whence, at five o' clock on Friday, we leave for Grenada. After that last blow one can re-read « The Thousand and One Nights ».

I read in a book that there are families here who, adown the centuries I am travelling in bad company, still preserve their title-deeds to properties in Spain and the keys of their houses.

Say « Bonjour » for me, Rue de la Pompe [3], and accept yourself my heartfelt greetings.

DEGAS.

To DE VALERNES [4].

Paris, October 26 (1890).

My dear de Valernes,

Constantly and with the deepest affection have I been thinking of you and yet did not write.

Your splendid letter reached me here in a little village named Diénay, in the Côte-d'Or, where we were, Bartholomé and I, through the following adventure :

On leaving you, after Geneva, I rejoined the said faithful friend at Dijon, whence we travelled to the said Diénay to see the Jeanniots, who live there a third of the year; and, after leaving them and once more in Paris, the recollection of the pleasures of that spot and the desire to make better acquaintance with admirable

---

1. The celebrated lyric artiste who created Ernest Reyer's *Sigurd* and *Salammbo,* and whose finest rôles were : Elisabeth *(Tannhauser)*, Elsa *(Lohengrin)*, Iphigénie *(Iphigénie en Tauride)* and Orphée.

2. Jacques Emile Blanche.

3. Where the Marquis de Fleury, brother of the first Mme Bartholomé lived.

4. A painter and friend of Degas.

Burgundy raised me to such a state of perambulatory excitement that I persuaded my good comrade to share my folly.

And that folly, now translated by us and others into particularly wise actions, could only be appeased by the hiring of a tilbury and a white horse, and the covering in twenty days (including five at Diénay when resting) of more than 600 kilomètres, or 150 leagues.

When the fine weather returns we shall start again with another horse (this one is too weak on its forelegs) and the same sort of carriage; and we shall perhaps go as far as the Rue Salodet [1], to stir your old heart once more, to inspect again your philosopher's home, your museum, your studio, and also to introduce you to Bartholomé, to whom I speak so often concerning your strenuous and tender life. All this will terrify you. But you will not have the courage to tell me that you are frightened. We will leave or not leave the animal in its stable at the Hôtel de l'Univers, and we will take you on with us to Avignon to see your « Sainte Thérèse » (it is in the Musée, is it not?), to talk about Delacroix and everything which is capable (that is the art it is our duty to exercise) of bewitching Truth and giving it the appearance of Folly.

You re-appear to me again, you and your little studio, where I seemed to make too rapid an inspection. My vision is as clear as though everything were before me. I have forgotten nothing; your two phases of life appear to me once more (less distinct than you thought and as I thought also). You have always, old friend, been the same man. There has ever persisted in you that delicious Romanticism which clothes and colours Truth, gives it that air of Folly which, as I have just said, is so good.

I am going to ask your pardon in this letter for something which often occurs in your conversation and more often in your mind : for having, in the course of our long artistic relations, been or had the appearance of being too « hard » with you.

I am singularly hard towards myself, as you must well recall, since you were led to reproach me for it and were astonished that I had so little self-confidence. I was or seemed to be hard towards everybody, in consequence of a sort of training in brutality, due to my doubts and bad temper. I felt myself to be so badly constructed, so wretchedly equipped, so flabby, whereas it seemed as though my « calculations » as regards art were so correct. I sulked with everybody, myself included. I beg your pardon if, on account of this cursed art, I wounded your most noble and most intelligent mind, perhaps even your heart.

That picture of « La Malade » [2], in which I can still see not only the effect as a whole and its so simply

expressed character of misfortune, but also the least stroke of your brush in its execution (as Duranty [3], might have said), is a fine picture.

The composition of these two women of Arles [4], the way they are grouped, is delicious.

I find that you still possess the same strong mind, the same firm and steady hand; and I envy you your eyes, which will enable you to see everything until the last day. Mine will not give me that joy. I can hardly read a scrap of the newspaper and, in the morning, on arriving at my studio, if I commit the stupidity of tarrying a little over that deciphering, I can no longer get to my work.

Recollect that you must count on my keeping you company when the time comes. Write to me.

With much love.   DEGAS.

To DURAND-RUEL.

Undated (Post-mark 1908).

Monsieur Durand-Ruel,

As usual, I am counting on you for the 15th. Have the kindness to set aside 2000 francs for me and send them tomorrow, Tuesday.

In the presence of the model, I did not dare to mention money to you yesterday.   DEGAS.

To ALEXIS ROUART.

August 21 (Post-mark 1908).

My dear Friend,

Do not be angry with me for so tardy a reply to your kind letter. I shall soon be a blind man.

Where there is no fish, it is useless being a fisherman. And just think of this, I would become a sculptor!

Good health to both of you.   DEGAS.

---

3. Duranty, Louis Emile Edmond (1833-1880), an art-critic and novelist, a disciple of Champfleury and, with him, one of the chief representatives of the Realist movement. He published several novels between 1860 and 1878, the first bearing the title « Le malheur d'Henriette Gérard». He has been reproached for the aridness of his composition and a disdain for any form of virtuosity, but these were perhaps the reasons for Degas' admiration for him.

In 1870, Duranty published through Dentu a pamphlet entitled « La nouvelle peinture, à propos du groupe d'artistes qui expose dans les Galeries Durand-Ruel ». Here he defines with great clearness and perfect comprehension the characteristics and tendancies of the new school of painting, and the evolution which the art of his time was undergoing. This pamphlet alone assures him a leading position as an art-critic (*vide* : « Degas as viewed by his critics », in the present work).

Degas painted an admirable portrait of Duranty, seated at his desk, facing the shelves of his library; a portrait painted in turpentine and dated 1879, and which, under the No. 48, was sold at the first sale of the works in Degas' studio for 95,000 francs. It is now in the W. Burelle collection, at Rozelle Alloway, Ayrshire (Scotland).

4. « Les deux Arlésiennes » belongs to Mme veuve Guigne, at Carpentras.

---

1. At Carpentras, where De Valernes lived.

2. This picture is in the Musée de Carpentras with the title « La Convalescente ».

30

BIBLIOGRAPHY

DEGAS : Vingt dessins, 1861-1896, published by Boussod Manzi, Joyant et Cie. — LIEBERMANN, M. : Degas, Berlin, Cassirer, 1899 (New edition in 1912). — LEMOISNE, P.-A. : Degas, l'Art de notre temps, Paris (1912). — GRAPPE, G. : Degas, L'Art et le Beau, Paris, (1911. — DETEIL, L. : Edgar Degas, Le peintre graveur illustré, Paris, 1919. — FOSCA, F. : Degas, Paris, Société des Trente, 1921. — DEGAS : Sedici opere di Degas, No IV, 1 series Maestri Moderni, Firenze, 1914. — VOLLARD, A. : Degas (1834-1917), Paris, Crès, 1924. — MEIER-GRAFFE, J. : Degas, München, 1920. — GUERIN, M. : Dix-neuf portraits de Degas par lui-même, Paris, Marcel Guérin, 1931. — GRAPPE, G. : Degas, Paris, Plon, s.d. (1936). — EXPOSITION DEGAS : 12 avril-2 mai 1924, Paris, Ed. des Galeries Georges Petit; introduction par Daniel Halévy, catalogue de Marcel Guérin. — DEGAS : 98 reproductions signées par Degas, Galerie Vollard, 1914 (Ed. Bernheim Jeune, 1918). — LAFOND, P. : Degas, Paris, Floury, 2 vol., 1918-1919. — HERTZ, H. : Degas, Paris, Alcan, 1920. — FOSCA, F. : Degas, les Albums d'art Druet, Paris, 1927. — ANDRÉ, A. : Degas, Pastels et dessins, Paris, Braun, 30 pl., 1934. — GAUFFIN, A. : Degas, utställning, national museum sal för tillfälliga utställningar, 23 januari-13 februari, Stockholm, 1920. — HOPPE, R. : Degas, Stockholm, 1922. — Mc ILHENNY : Exposition Degas, Préface de I.-P. Sachs, introd. by A. Mongan, Pennsylvania Museum of Art, Philadelphie, 1936. —COQUIOT, G. : Degas, Paris, Ollendorff, 1924. — LETTRES DE DEGAS : recueillies et annotées par Marcel Guérin, préface de Daniel Halévy, Paris, Bernard Grasset, 1931. — RIVIÈRE, H. : Degas, Les dessins des grands artistes français, Paris, Demotte, 1922-1923. — JAMOT, P. : Degas, Paris, *Gazette des Beaux-Arts,* 1924. — MANSON, J.-B. : The life and work of Edgar Degas, London, 1927. — RIVIÈRE, G. : M. Degas, bourgeois de Paris, Paris, Floury, 1935. — EXPOSITION DEGAS : mars-avril 1937, Paris, introd. by Paul Jamot, catalogue by Mmes Bouchot-Saupique and Delaroche-Vernet. — GEFFROY, G. : Histoire de l'impressionnisme (3d series of La Vie Artistique), Paris, Dentu, 1894. — DURANTY : La nouvelle peinture, Paris, Dentu, 1876. — BERALDY, H. : Les graveurs du XIXe siècle, 1886, vol. V. — BRICON, E. : Psychologie d'art, les Maîtres de la fin du XIXe siècle, Paris, 1900. — THIIS, JENS : Norske Malere og Billedhuggere, Bergen, 1904. — BLANCHE, J.-E. : Propos de peintres, de David à Degas, Paris, Emile, Paul 1919. — MAUCLAIR, C. : Les Maîtres de l'Impressionnisme, Paris, Ollendorff (1923). — HUYSMANS, J.-K. : L'art moderne, Paris, 1883 (New edition 1902). — MARCEL, H. : La peinture française au XIXe siècle, Paris, 1905. — THIEME-BECKER : Allgemeines Lexicon der Bildenden Künste, vol. VIII, 1913. — DURET, T. : Critique d'avant-garde, Paris, Charpentier, 1885. — HUYSMANS, J.-K. : Certains, Paris, Tresse et Stock, 1889. — SALMON, A. : Propos d'atelier, Paris, Crès, 1922. — BASTLER ET KUNSTLER : La peinture indépendante en France, t. I, de Monet à Bonnard, Paris, 1929, in-8o. — LEROY, A. : Histoire de la peinture française (1800-1933), son évolution et ses maîtres, Paris, 1934. — FÉNÉON, F. : Les impressionnistes en 1886, Paris, *La Vogue,* 1886. — LECOMTE, G. : L'art impressionniste, Paris, Chamerot et Renouard, 1892. — MOORE, G. : Modern painting, London, 1893. — MOORE, G. : Confessions d'un jeune Anglais, Paris, Stock, 1925. — REY, R. : La peinture française à la fin du XIXe siècle; la renaissance du sentiment classique, Paris, 1931. — JAMOT, P. : La peinture en France, Paris, 1934. — SCHMIDT, K.-E. : Französische Malerei des XIX. Jahrh., Leipzig, 1903. MIREUR : Dictionnaire des ventes d'art, II, 1902. — MAUCLAIR, C. : L'Impressionnisme, son histoier, son esthétique, ses maîtres, Paris, Librairie de l'art ancien et moderne, 1903. — KLINGSOR, T. : La peinture française depuis vingt ans, Rieder, 1921. — WALDMANN, E. : Die Kunst des Realismus und des Impressionismus, Berlin, 1927. — FAURE, E. : Histoire de l'art, l'Art moderne, Paris, 1926. — GONCOURT, E. (de) : Mémoires de la vie littéraire, Paris, Fasquelle, 9 vol. — LAFORGUE, J. : Œuvres complètes, III, Mélanges posthumes, Paris, 1903. — MEIER-GRAEFE, J. Entwicklungsgeschichte der Modernen Kunst, Munich, 1915. — MIGEON, G., JAMOT, P., VITRY, P., DREYFUS, C. : La collection Isaac de Carmondo au Musée du Louvre, Paris, *Gazette des Beaux-Arts,* Bruxelles, Ed. Van Oest, 1914. — RÉAU, L. : Chapitre de l'histoire de l'art d'André Michel, 1926. — MICHEL, A. : Sur la peinture française au XIXe siècle, Paris, 1928. — MUTHER, R. : History of Modern Painting, London, 4 vol., 1907. — BLANCHE, J.-E. : Les arts plastiques sous la IIIe République, Paris, Editions de France, 1931. — FOCILLON, H. : La peinture au XIXe et XXe siècle, du Réalisme à nos jours, Paris, 1928. — MEIER-GRAEFE, J. : Der Moderne Impressionnismus, IIe édition, Berlin, 1904. — FIERENS-GEVAERT : Nouveaux essais sur l'art contemporain, Paris, Alcan, 1903. — MAC COLL, D. S. : Nineteenth Century Art, Glasgow, 1902. — MOORE, G. : Impressions and opinions. — MELLERIO, A. L'exposition de 1900 et l'impressionnisme, Paris, Floury, 1900. — PICA, V. : Edgar Degas, Emporium, décembre 1907. — WALDMANN, E. : Toulouse-Lautrec et Degas, Die Graphischen Künste, 1911, II. — BÉNÉDITE, L. : La réorganisation du Luxembourg, Revue encyclopédique, August 28th 1897. — CHARLES, E. : Les mots de Degas, Renaissance de l'art français, April 1918. — MOORE, G. : Memories of Degas, Burlington Magazine, January-February 1918. — BÉNÉDITE, L. : La peinture française, l'Art et les artistes, 1911 — MELLERIO, A. : Degas, Revue Artistique, April 1896. — MARX, R. : Exposition chez Durand-Ruel, Revue encyclopédique, 1896. — MARX, R. : Degas, L'Image, octobre 1897. — MAUCLAIR, C. : Edgar Degas, Revue de l'art ancien et moderne, 1903. — MOORE, G. : Edgar Degas, The Magazine of Art, 1900. — LECOMTE, G. : La crise de la peinture française, L'Art et les artistes, 1910. — GEFFROY, G. : Degas, L'Art et les artistes 1908. — SICKERT, W. : Degas, Burlington Magazine, November 1917. — GSELL, P. : Edgar Degas statuaire, Renaissance de l'art français, December, 1918. — LEMOISNE, P.-A. : Les statuettes de Degas, Art et Décoration, 1919. — LEMOISNE, P.-A. : Les carnets de Degas au Cabinet des Estampes, *Gazette des Beaux-Arts,* 1921. — GUÉRIN, M. : Note sur les monotypes de Degas, Amour de l'Art, 1924. — HAUSENSTEIN, W. : Degas, Die Kunst, 1925. — LEMOISNE, P.-A. : Le portrait de Degas par lui-même, Beaux-Arts, December 1st, 1927. — BLANCHE, J.-E. : Portrait de Degas, Formes, February 1931. — ROMANELLI, R. : Cézanne et Degas, Belvédère, January 1930. — LETTRES DE DEGAS, Kunst und Künstler, 1932. — MELLERIO, A. : Un album de reproduction d'après les dessins de M. Degas, L'Estampe et l'Affiche, 1898. — MOORE, G. : Degas, Kunst und Künstler, VI. — HOURTICQ, L. : Edgar Degas, Art et Décoraion, October 1912. — GAUGUIN, M. : Degas, Kunst und Künstler, March 1912. — ALEXANDRE, A. : Degas graveur et lithographe, Les Arts, No 171, 1918. — GUÉRIN, M. : Remarque sur les portraits de famille peints par Degas, *Gazette des Beaux-Arts,* June 1928. — TROENDLE, H. : Die Tradition im Werke Degas, Kunst und Künstler, 1926. — LEMOISNE, P.-A. : Degas, Revue de l'Art, June 1924. — MONGAN, A. : Degas master observer : seen at Philadelphia, The Art News, 1936. — VALÉRY, P. : A propos de Degas, Mesures et Nouvelle Revue française, October 1935. — ROUART, E. : Degas, Le Point, February 1937, suivi de : Degas — Degas, le réalisme et Duranty. — MOREAU-NELATON, E. : Deux heures avec Degas, interview posthume, Amour de l'Art, 1931. — HUYGHE, R. : Degas ou la fiction réaliste, Amour de l'Art, 1931 — BAZIN, G. : Degas sculpteur, Amour de l'Art, 1931. — BAZIN, G. : Degas et l'objectif, Amour de l'Art, 1931. — PICENI, E. : « Degas, nomo cattivo », l'Illustrazione italiana, 1932. — WALKER, J. : Degas et les maîtres anciens, *Gazette des Beaux-Arts,* 1933. — CHIALIVA : Comment Degas a changé sa technique du dessin, Bulletin Art français, 1932. — PAULSON, G. : L'Exposition Degas à Stockholm, Stenmans Konstrevy, mai 1920. — VALÉRY, P. : Degas, Revue hebdomadaire, 1920. — JAMOT, P. : Degas, peintre d'assiettes, *Gazette des Beaux-Arts,* 1924. — HERTZ, H. : Degas coloriste, Amour de l'Art, 1904. — GLASER, CURT : Degas statuaire, Kunst und Künstler, 1922. — DAYOT, A. : Edgar Degas, la Revue Rhénane. — VOLLARD, A. : Conversations with Degas, The Arts, 1924. — BLANCHE, J.-E. : Bartholomé et Degas, Art vivant, 1930. — VITRY, P. : L'exposition Degas à l'Orangerie, Bulletin des Musées de France, 1931. — JAMOT, P. : Une salle Degas au Louvre, Amour de l'Art, 1931. — LETTRES DE DEGAS: Amour de l'Art, 1931.

SELF-PORTRAIT OF THE ARTIST
Photo Hyperion

A SELF-PORTRAIT
Photo Floury

PORTRAIT OF DEGAS AND THE PAINTER VALERNES
Photo Arch. Phot. d'Art et d'Histoire

HALF-LENGTH PORTRAIT OF A MAN
Photo Durand-Ruel

PORTRAIT OF HILAIRE DEGAS, THE ARTIST'S GRANDFATHER
Photo Arch. Phot. d'Art et d'Histoire

PORTRAITS OF ALEXIS AND HENRI ROUART
Photo Durand-Ruel

PORTRAITS OF AUGUSTE DEGAS — THE ARTIST'S FATHER — AND
THE GUITARIST PAGANS
Photo Arch. Phot. d'Art et d'Histoire

PORTRAIT OF DIEGO MARTELLI
Photo Hyperion

A PORTRAIT GROUP: WALTER SICKERT, DANIEL HALÉVY, LUDOVIC
HALÉVY, J.-E. BLANCHE, GERVEX AND BOULANGER CAVÉ.

PORTRAIT OF EUGÈNE MANET
Photo Floury

A WOMAN READING
Photo Durand-Ruel

A YOUNG WOMAN WITH RED HAIR
Photo Durand-Ruel

HALF-LENGTH PORTRAIT OF A WOMAN
Photo Durand-Ruel

PORTRAIT OF A YOUNG WOMAN SEATED AGAINST A BACKGROUND
OF CHRYSANTHEMUMS
Photo Durand-Ruel

PORTRAIT OF MADEMOISELLE MALO
Photo Durand-Ruel

PORTRAIT OF THE DUCHESSE DE MORBILLI
Photo Arch. Photo d'Art et d'Histoire

PORTRAIT OF MADEMOISELLE DOBIGNY
Photo Hyperion

PORTRAIT OF MADEMOISELLE SALLE
Photo Floury

HEAD OF A WOMAN
Photo Arch. Photo d'Art et d'Histoire

A WOMAN OF SAVOY
Photo Durand-Ruel

PORTRAIT OF MADAME FÈVRE
Photo Floury

THE BELLELI FAMILY
Phot. Arch. Phot. d'Art et d'Histoire

A STUDY OF HANDS FOR THE PORTRAITS OF THE BELLELI FAMILY

Photo Arch. Phot. d'Art et d'Histoire

PORTRAIT OF GIOVANNINA BELLELI
Phot. Arch. Phot. d'Art et d'Histoire

STUDY FOR THE PORTRAIT OF THE BELLELI FAMILY
Photo Durand-Ruel

A BEGGAR-WOMAN IN ROME
Photo Durand-Ruel

HEAD OF A YOUNG WOMAN
Photo Floury

POUTING
Photo Durand-Ruel

THE CONVERSATION
Photo Durand-Ruel

AN OLD ITALIAN WOMAN
Photo Durand-Ruel

THE CONVERSATION
Photo Durand-Ruel

A WOMAN WITH A PINK HAT (PORTRAIT OF MADAME D. M.)
Photo Durand-Ruel

A. WOMAN IN A CAFÉ
Photo Hyperion

PORTRAIT OF MADAME GOBILLARD-MORISOT
Photo Floury

THE DUCHESSE DE MONTEJASI-CICERALE WITH HER DAUGHTERS (Detail)
Photo Arch. Phot. d'Art et d'Histoire

YOUNG SPARTANS EXERCISING ·
Photo Durand-Ruel

THE RAPE OF THE SABINES (after Poussin)
Photo Floury

THE MISFORTUNES OF THE CITY OF ORLEANS
Photo Arch. Phot. d'Art et d'Histoire

SEMIRAMIS BUILDING A TOWN
Photo Floury

PORTRAIT OF MADEMOISELLE FIOCRE IN THE BALLET "LA SOURCE"
Photo Arch. Phot. d'Art et d'Histoire

A COTTON BUREAU IN NEW-ORLEANS
Photo Floury

TWO YOUNG WOMEN IN A PICTURE-GALLERY
Photo Durand-Ruel

ABSINTHE
Photo Floury

A CAFÉ ON THE BOULEVARD MONTMARTRE
Photo Floury

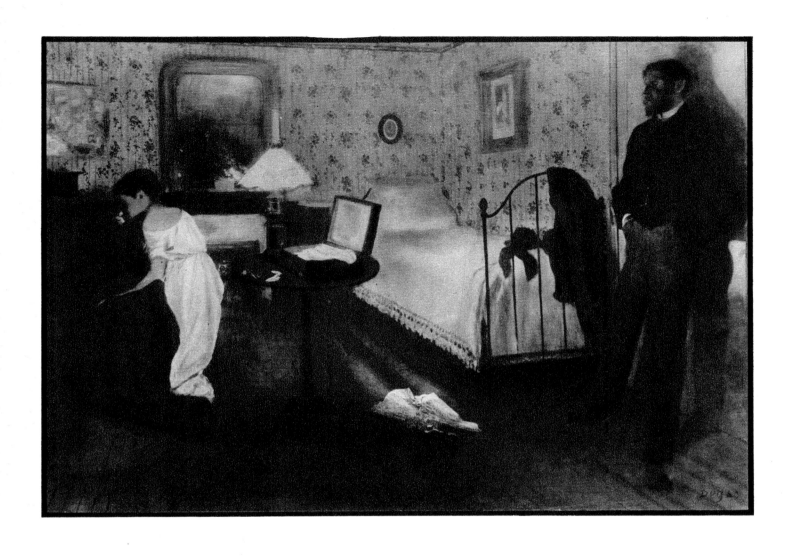

AN INTERIOR SCENE (also entitled " THE RAPE ")
Photo Durand-Ruel

A FALSE START
Photo Durand-Ruel

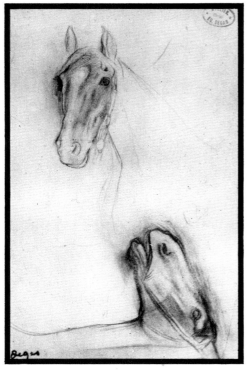

A RACE-COURSE STUDY
Photo Durand-Ruel

AT THE RACES
Photo Durand-Ruel

AT THE RACES (GENTLEMEN-RIDERS)
Photo Hyperion

RACE-HORSES
Photo Durand-Ruel

THE PARADE BEFORE THE GRANDSTAND
Photo Durand-Ruel

CARRIAGE AT THE RACES
Photo Durand-Ruel

AT THE RACES : BEFORE THE START
Photo Durand-Ruel

HOUSES AT THE BASE OF A CLIFF
Photo Durand-Ruel

MISS CASSATT IN A PICTURE-GALLERY
Photo Floury

WOMEN DRESSING THEIR HAIR
Photo Druet

WOMAN AND CHRYSANTHEMUMS
Photo Hyperion

WOMAN DRESSING HER HAIR
Photo Durand-Ruel

THE TOILET
Photo Druet

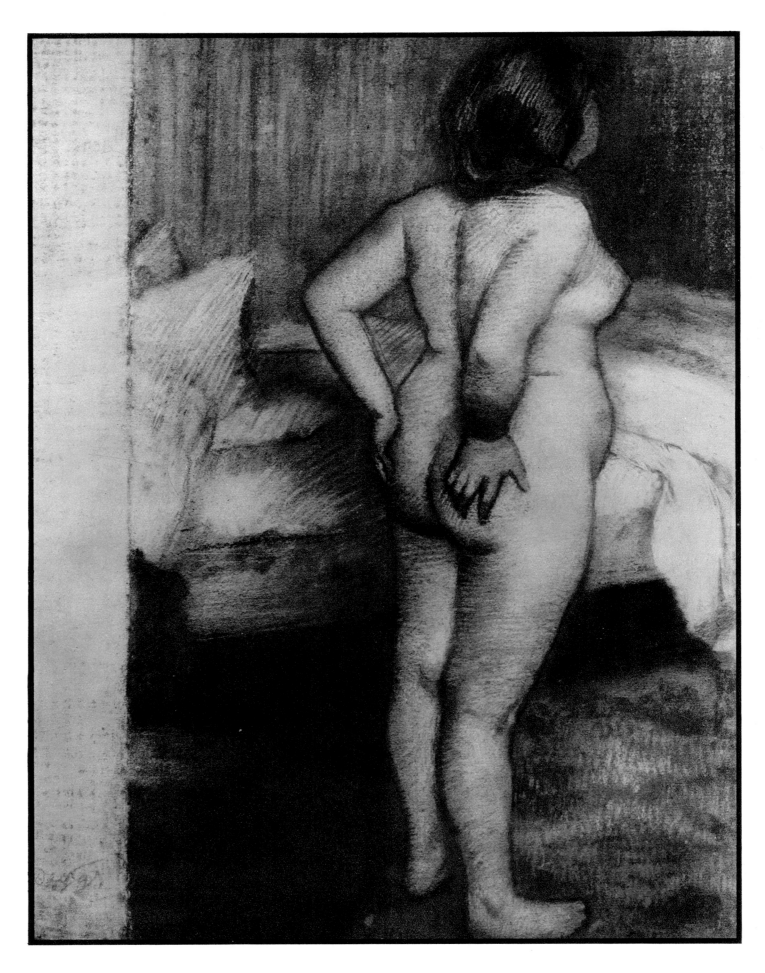

A STUDY OF THE NUDE
Photo Druet

AFTER THE BATH
Photo Durand-Ruel

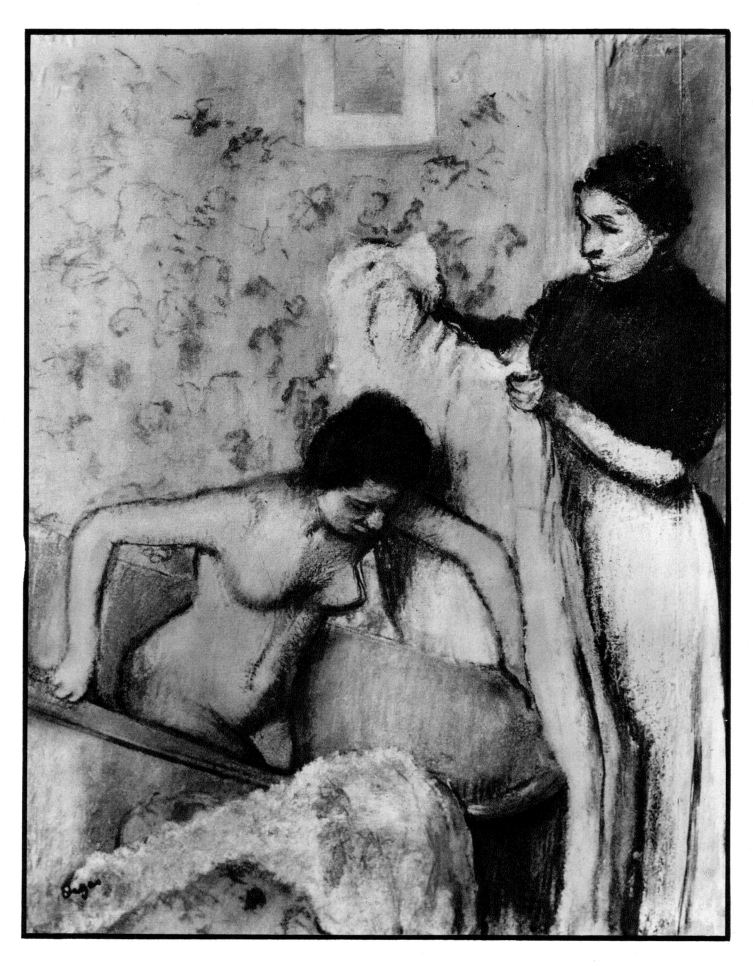

AFTER THE BATH
Photo Durand-Ruel

THE PEDICURE
Photo Durand-Ruel

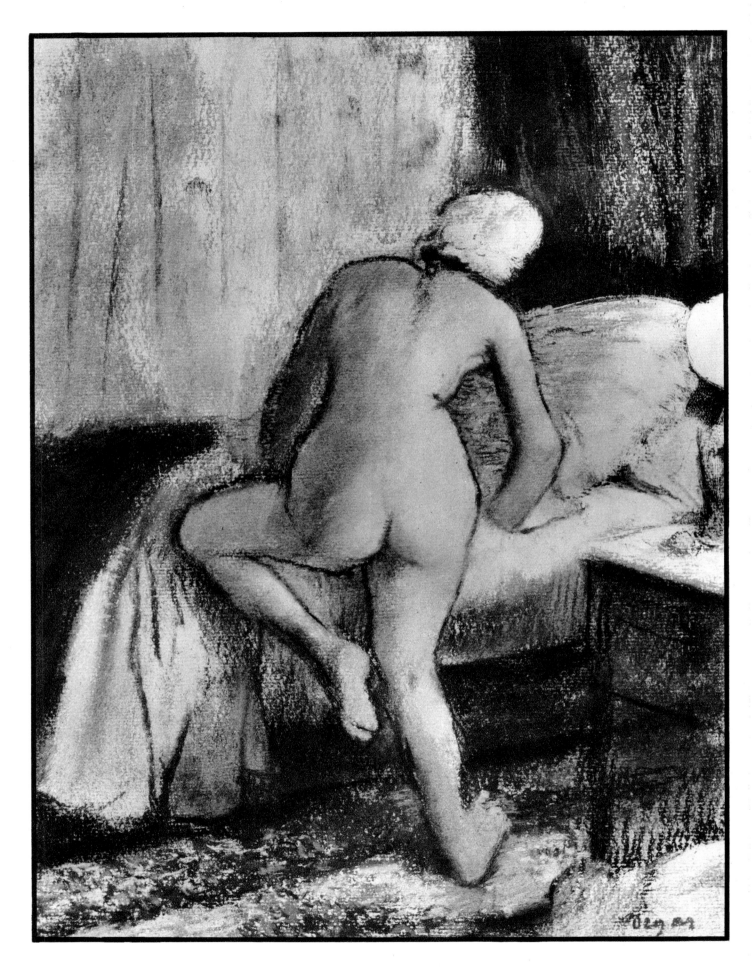

BED-TIME
Photo Durand-Ruel

AFTER THE BATH
Photo Hyperion

A WOMAN IN HER BATH-TUB
Photo Durand-Ruel

THE TOILET
Photo Durand-Ruel

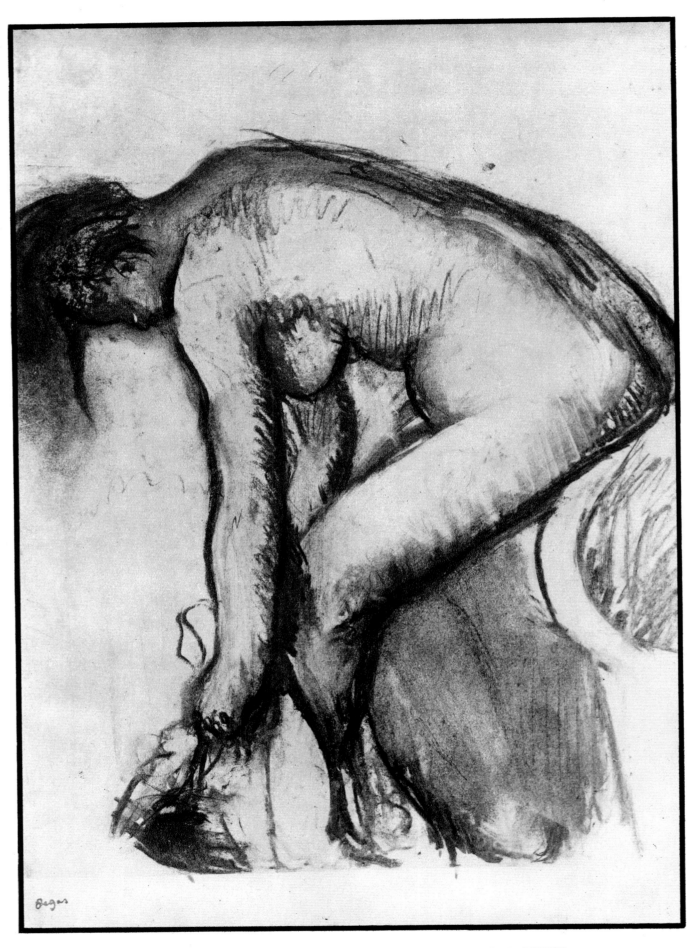

AFTER THE BATH : A WOMAN DRYING HER FEET
Photo Durand-Ruel

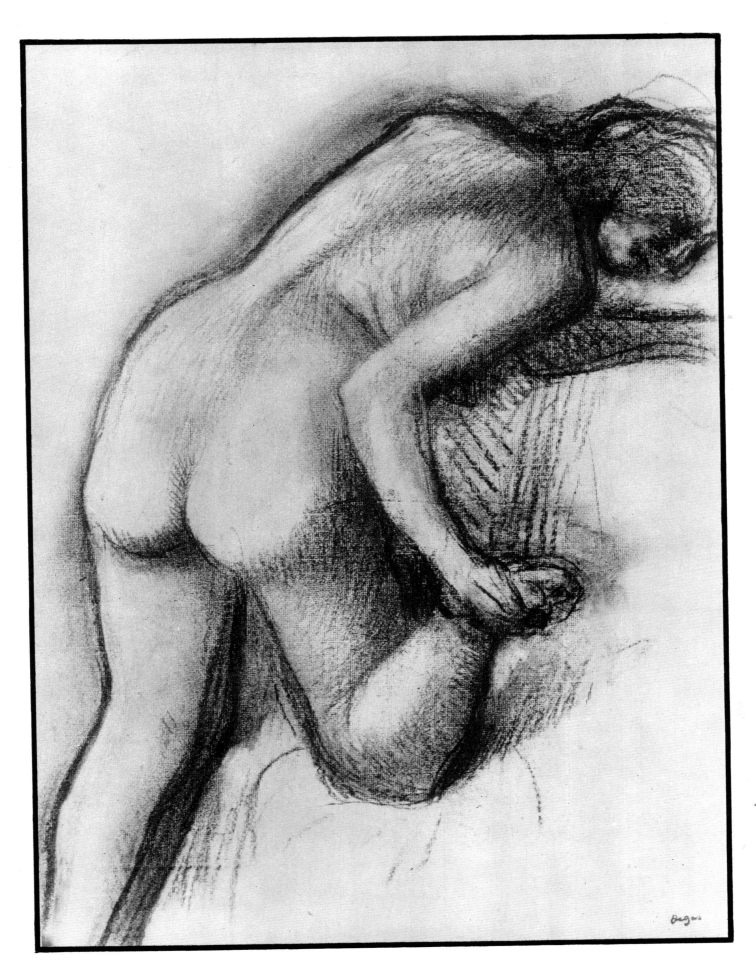

A STUDY OF THE NUDE
Photo Durand-Ruel

WOMAN IN HER BATH-TUB
Photo Arch. Phot. d'Art et d'Histoire

THE TOILET
Photo Durand-Ruel

THE SONG OF THE DOG
Photo Floury

A CAFÉ-CONCERT (" LES AMBASSADEURS „)
Photo Hyperion

THE SINGER IN GREEN
Photo Durand-Ruel

A SINGER WITH A GLOVE
Photo Durand-Ruel

WOMAN IRONING
Photo Durand-Ruel

WOMAN IRONING
Photo Durand-Ruel

WOMEN IRONING
Photo Durand-Ruel

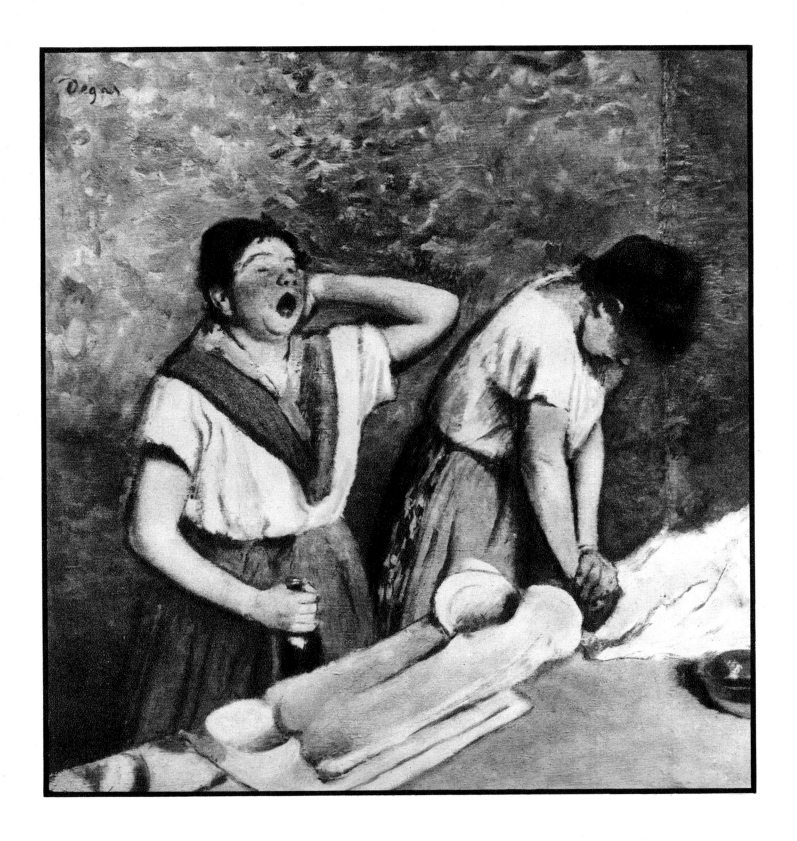

WOMEN IRONING
Photo Durand-Ruel

THE MILLINER
Photo Durand-Ruel

MILLINERS
Photo Hyperion

A MILLINER'S WORK-ROOM
Photo Hyperion

PORTRAIT OF MADÁME JEANTEAUD LOOKING AT HERSELF IN A MIRROR
Photo Floury

DANCING-GIRLS AT REST
Photo Durand-Ruel

WAITING
Photo Durand-Ruel

DANCING-GIRL IN HER DRESSING-ROOM
Photo Durand-Ruel

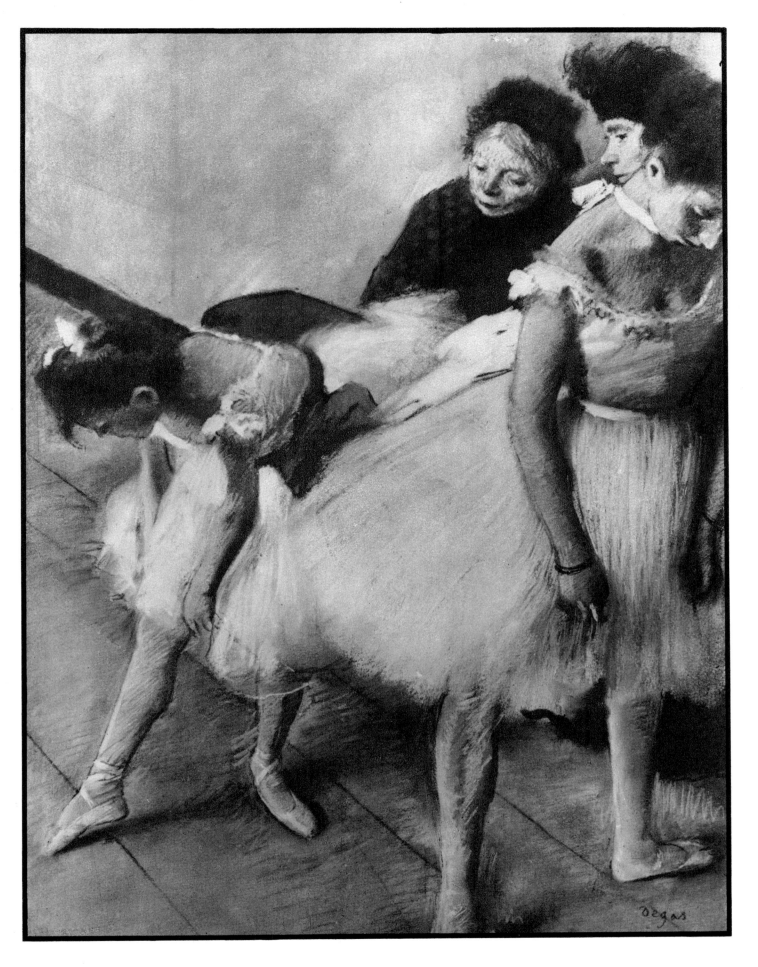

DANCING-GIRLS ARRANGING THEIR TOILET
Photo Durand-Ruel

DANCING-GIRL IN HER DRESSING-ROOM
Photo Floury

DANCING-GIRLS BEHIND THE FRAMEWORK OF A FLAT
Photo Hyperion

THE DANCING-LESSON IN THE GREEN-ROOM
Photo Durand-Ruel

THE DANCING-REHEARSAL
Photo Durand-Ruel

REST-TIME
Photo Durand-Ruel

DANCING-GIRL AT THE PHOTOGRAPHER'S
Photo Durand-Ruel

THE REHEARSAL IN THE GREEN-ROOM
Photo Durand-Ruel

REHEARSAL OF A BALLET ON THE STAGE
Photo Durand-Ruel

THE DANCING LESSON
Photo Durand-Ruel

THE DANCING-LESSON
Photo Hyperion

THE DANCING-LESSON WITH VIOLONIST
Photo Durand-Ruel

MISS LALA AT THE FERNANDO CIRCUS
Photo Durand-Ruel

HALF-LENGTH STUDIES OF DANCING-GIRLS
Photo Durand-Ruel

HALF-LENGTH STUDIES OF DANCING-GIRLS
Photo Durand-Ruel

THREE DANCING-GIRLS
Photo Durand-Ruel

DANCING-GIRL RE-ARRANGING HER SHOULDER-STRAP
Photo Durand-Ruel

RUSSIAN DANCING-GIRLS
Photo Hyperion

HALF-LENGTH STUDIES OF DANCING-GIRLS
Photo Hyperion

THE DANCING-GIRL IN GREEN
Photo Durand-Ruel

DANCING-GIRL
Photo Durand-Ruel

THE CLOSE OF AN ARABESQUE
Photo Floury

DANCING-GIRL PIROUETTING
Photo Durand-Ruel

THE BALLET
Photo Durand-Ruel

STARS OF THE BALLET
Photo Floury

THE OPERATIC STAR
Photo Floury

DANCING-GIRL THANKING HER AUDIENCE
Photo Hyperion

DANCING-GIRLS
Photo Durand-Ruel

ENTRANCE ON THE STAGE OF MASKED DANCERS
Photo Durand-Ruel

TWO DANCING-GIRLS PRACTISING AT THE BAR
Photo Durand-Ruel

DANCING-GIRLS PRACTISING AT THE BAR
Photo Durand-Ruel

THREE DANCING-GIRLS
Photo Durand-Ruel

DANCING-GIRLS
Photo Durand-Ruel

DANCING-GIRLS
Photo Durand-Ruel

DANCING-GIRLS IN BLUE
Photo Hyperion

A BALLET SCENE
Photo Durand-Ruel

MUSICIANS IN THE ORCHESTRA
Photo Durand-Ruel

THE SUPERNUMERARIES
Photo Floury

REST-TIME
Photo Hyperion

THE BOX
Photo Durand-Ruel

THE ORCHESTRA
Photo Arch. Phot. d'Art et d'Histoire

THE BALLET OF "ROBERT LE DIABLE"
Photo Durand-Ruel

DEGAS AS VIEWED BY HIS CRITICS

TO all those who have a passionate love for pictures, nothing is more interesting and at the same time so instructive as to search for the history of the progress of a great artist from the time when he made his first efforts to attain celebrity. It is by turning over the leaves of old books and ancient periodicals (sometimes ephemeral publications, now so rare that bibliophiles and art critics search for them with avidity) that we can follow not merely the stages of a life devoted to art, we can also reconstruct the atmosphere of an epoque of the past, with, on the one hand, the prejudices — even the hatred — of certain writers and, on the other, the perspicacity of those who did not hesitate to uphold, against an official school and a public both incapable of recognizing genius, that a painter with an extraordinarily clear vision had made his appearance in the world of art and was about to lay the foundations of a veritable æsthetic revolution. This method of studying the history of art is above all profitable in the case of the artists of the so-called Impressionist School, and certainly when applying it to the artistic career of a Degas our task becomes truly fascinating.

As though an official interdict had been issued against Edgar Degas (1834-1917), this master was for a long time ignored by those who selected works for the Luxembourg Gallery. Nevertheless, according to many art critics during the years 1874-1880, he possessed remarkable titles of nobility. From the year 1874, M. Claretie placed him at the head of the new school; M. Gonse, attracted by his pastels at the Salon of 1877, by his « studies of dancing-girls in the green-room, most remarkable from the point of view of gesture and mimicry », regarded him as « an artist of much greater talent than he wished to appear; one not unworthy of the great traditions of La Tour and Chardin »; whilst, under the date of February 13, 1874, Edmond de Goncourt, who had a fondness for setting down Degas' witticisms, gave, in his *Mémoires de la vie littéraire,* a most curious account of a visit he paid to the painter, at his studio.

« Yesterday, I spent my afternoon in the studio of an artist named Degas... », he writes. « After many endeavours... he has set his heart upon laundry-women and dancing-girls. I cannot imagine a better choice, since I myself, in *Manette Salomon,* have extolled these two professions as supplying a modern artist with the most pictorial models among the women of to-day. Indeed, we find there flesh-pink side by side with snow-white linen, or mingled with the milky haze of gauze : the most charming pretext for blond and tender colouring. »

And the great novelist continues to add words which are of considerable importance to those who seek to know Degas and his art thoroughly.

« This Degas is an original fellow », he notes to the extent of two pages which deserve to be read in their entirety. « He is a morbid and neurotic chap, an ophtalmic subject to such an extent that he fears to lose his eye-sight... Will he ever accomplish anything absolutely complete? I cannot say. He appears to me to be of very uneasy mind. ». A baseless fear, since, in 1880, the *Gazette des Beaux-Arts* saw in him a « pupil of the great Florentine painters, of Lorenzo di Credi and Ghirlandajo, and above all the pupil of a great Frenchman, M. Ingres ».

Among the earliest articles in the Parisian press on Degas, I must also draw attention to a fanciful contribution to *Le Charivari* of April 25, 1874, from the pen of Louis Leroy. His subject was the Impressionist Exhibition — the first which was held on the Boulevard des Capucines, and in a most amusing manner he gives the impressions of an imaginary member of the official school of painting — a certain « Monsieur Joseph Vincent, a pupil of Bertin », who, naturally, was horrified when brought face to face with the revolutionary art of Pissaro, Sisley, Monet, Cézanne, Renoir and Manet. Paradoxically « Le Père Vincent » had a few amiable words to say about Degas. « He uttered cries of horror before each picture; it was only the horrible that attracted him, since Degas' badly washed *Washerwoman* caused him to utter cries of admiration... Before every other picture and in the presence of the caretaker he began to dance the scalp-dance! »

But much more important than this humorous article is a very rare publication of 1877, — *L'Impressionniste : Journal d'Art,* published during the Exhibition of that year at 22bis, Rue Laffitte, under the editorship of G. Rivière, who wrote most of the articles and notes, with the collaboration of « Un peintre », who is said to have been Renoir. Only five issues (each of eight pages, at the price of 15 centimes) were published, evidently as propaganda for Degas, Renoir, Caillebotte, Sisley (whose name is printed as Sizley) and other painters of the « Impressionist » school. Apart from the text, this little journal contains some curious sketches by Degas (a *Danseuse à la barre,* a very rudimentary but expressive sketch in line), Renoir, Sisley and Caillebotte.

In his first number, Rivière deplores the ignorance of art critics when brought face to face with the *nouvelle peinture* : « they have seen nothing, neither the astounding drawing, nor the charming, youthful colouring of M. Renoir... nor the science and grandeur of MM. Cézanne and Degas... They laughed, after the fashion of ignorant and pretentious folk... »

Writing on the subject of the whole Impressionists' Exhibition, held in the Rue Le Peletier, Rivière devotes a whole page of his journal to the « most astounding pictures by M. Degas — pictures hung in a little gallery at the end of the Grand Salon. — His works are always witty, delicate and sincere... His prodigious science declares itself spontaneously on all sides... He is an observer. »

More important still is a booklet of thirty-eight pages, published by Duranty in 1876, with the title *La Nouvelle peinture : A propos du groupe d'artistes qui expose dans les Galeries Durand-Ruel.* In this remarkable example of special-pleading for the Impressionists, no member of the group is named, but from his descriptions it is clear that Duranty had before his eyes this or that work by Manet, Whistler, Ribot, Bracquemont, and above all Degas, who was later, as we read in Joris Karl Huysmans' *L'Art Moderne* (1883), to depict Duranty and produce one of his finest portraits.

Having read *La Nouvelle Peinture,* where we learn that « the debate is truly only between ancient and modern art, between the old pictures and the new... the movement is already deeply enrooted... it has abandoned the old style... and come out into the open air and the sun... The origin of its efforts dates from the days of Courbet... we note those efforts in the case of the great Ingres and the mighty Millet... they are also to be found in the works of the great Corot and his disciple Chintreuil », — having read this disquisition regarding the conceptions of Degas and his friends, turn to the masterly description which Huysmans gives of the portrait of the celebrated Duranty.

« Monsieur Duranty is depicted », wrote Huysmans, « amidst his prints and books, seated at his table, and his slender, nervous fingers, his keen, mocking eye, his searching, piercing look, his expression as of an English comedian, and his dry little laugh within the stem of his pipe passed before me as I looked on this canvas on which the character of this curious analyst is so well rendered. »

The articles which Huysmans collected together in *L'Art Moderne* had already appeared in *Le Voltaire, La Réforme, La Revue littéraire et artistique,* and in a certain « feuille de chou» cùltivated by M. Bachelin-Deflorenne, *La Gazette des Amateurs,* in which he made his début as an art-critic with an article on Degas.

« The great qualities of this artist », writes Huysmans, « suddenly and in their entirety appeared to me. And the joy which I experienced as a youth has ever since then increased at each of the exhibitions to which Degas has contributed... A painter of modern life was born and one who springs from no one, who bears no resemblance to anyone, who brings an entirely new artistic flavour, and wholly new methods of execution. »

Once launched on the subject of the pictures of the Salon of 1879, Huysmans let his vitriolic pen flow on in the following characteristic manner :

« Ah! more interesting are these kill-joys, so detested and abused, the Independants. I do not deny that among them are some who do not know their profession sufficiently well. But take a man of great talent, like M. Degas, — take even his pupil, Mlle Mary Cassatt, — and see whether the works of these artists are not more interesting, more distinguished than all these jingling contrivances which hang from the line to the ceiling in the interminable rooms of the Exhibition. The fact is that, with them, I find a true regard for contemporary life , and M. Degas is, undoubtedly, among the painters who have followed the naturalist movement, brought about in painting by the Impressionists and Manet, the one who has remained the most original and boldest. He was one of the first to grapple with feminine and popular elegancies; one of the first he ventured to face artificial lightings, the glare of the footlights before which lightly clad singers or dancers in muslin bawl out their songs or pirouette.   In his works we find flesh which is neither creamy nor smooth, the very reverse of gold-beater's skin, it is real flesh powdered with *veloutine,* flesh with the make up of the stage and the alcove, exactly as it is, with its harsh granular texture when seen near to, and its sickly brilliancy when seen from afar.   Degas is a past-master in the art of rendering what I will readily name the « civilized carnation ».   He is also a past-master in the art of depicting woman-hood, of representing woman — no matter to what class of society she may belong — in all her pretty movements and graceful attitudes. »

From the point of view of Degas' palette, Huysmans often makes many instructive remarks. For instance, when writing on the subject of the portrait of Duranty, already referred to, he points out :

« The almost bright pink patches on the forehead, the green on the beard, the blue on the velvet of the sitter's collar; whilst the fingers are made up of yellow edged with bishop's violet.   Near to, it consists of a hatching of colours which are hammered out and split up and appear to encroach one on the other; but at a few paces everything is in harmony and melts into the exact flesh-tone, — flesh which palpitates and is alive, such as no one in France until now has known how to paint ».

Let me give yet another quotation from this great writer whom I had the privilege of knowing during my youth; because, long before other critics, my friend Joris Karl Huysmans had himself produced in literature the counterpart of the work of Degas in painting.

Writing on the subject of the Exhibition of the Independants in 1881, Huysmans says :

« M. Degas has shown himself singularly parsimonious.   He has satisfied himself by exhibit-ing a scene behind the scenes, — a gentleman pressing a woman to his bosom, almost pressing her legs between his thighs, behind the framework of a flat illuminated by the red glow from the audi-torium which one can just glimpse; — this work and a few drawings and sketches depicting singers on the stage extending their paws which move like those of wretched Saxony porcelaine figures and bestowing a blessing on the heads of the musicians, above which emerges, in the foreground, like an enormous figure five, the neck of a violoncelle, or else swaying their hips and bellowing amidst those inept convulsions which have procured almost celebrity for that epileptic doll — La Bécat. Add two more sketches : the faces of some criminals with animal-like mugs, low foreheads, promi-nent cheek-bones, receding chins, little furtive eyes, and a very astonishing feminine nude, at the end of the room, and you have the list of the drawings and paintings contributed by this artist. »

But wait a bit! — there was another work by Degas on view at that particular exhibition, — « the curiosity of his show of 1881 was a piece of sculpture, a statuette in wax, entitled *Petite dan-seuse de quatorze ans* », at the sight of which the alarmed and embarrassed public fled.

« The terrible reality of this statuette fills the public with a sickish feeling.   All its ideas regarding sculpture with its cold, inanimate whiteness, — the conventional work which has been copied again and again for centuries,— are overthrown.   The fact is that M. Degas has suddenly knocked the traditions of sculpture head over heels, just as he has for so long a time shaken the con-ventions regarding painting. »

Huysmans was very doubtful whether Degas would obtain « the slightest success » with his sculpture, — « no more than with his painting, the exquisiteness of which is unintelligible to the public, his most original and bold sculpture will not even be surmised ».

In 1882, neither Degas, nor his pupil Miss Cassatt, nor Raffaëlli, nor Forain, nor Zandoma-neghi exhibited with the Independants.   He had begun to shut himself up within his ivory tower. Far away indeed were the days, about 1865, when, at the Café Guerbois, on the Avenue de Clichy, the young painters and writers of the new epoch used to meet almost every evening to discuss æsthe-tics.   In that company there were Renoir, Manet, Cazin, Lhermitte, Pissarro, Whistler, Austruc and undoubtedly Degas.   But little by little Degas detached himself to work alone; and he exhibited less and less often.   The first exhibition of his group was at Nadar's, 35, Boulevard des Capucines, from April 15 to May 15; the seventh was held in April, 1882, in the Rue Saint-Honoré.   Side by side with Miss Cassatt, Caillebotte, Cézanne, Forain and the others, he exhibited in 1874, 1876, 1877, 1879, 1880, 1881, and, to finish, in 1886.

It was in 1886 that Félix Fénéon published his excellent booklet on « Les Impressionnistes en 1886 » (Paris, *La Vogue*), written on the occasion of the eighth Impressionist Exhibition, which was held at 1, Rue Laffitte, between May 15 and June 15. In his preface the author notes that neither Renoir nor Monet exhibited, but Degas was there with his characteristic contributions.

« In M. Degas' work — and in what other? », comments Félix Fénéon, « these human skins are intensely alive. The lines of this cruel and sagacious observer make clear, amidst difficulties of foreshortening which are wildly elliptic, the mechanism of every moment; in the case of a being in motion they register not only the essential gesture but also its slightest and most remote myological reactions. Hence that definite unity in draughtsmanship. It is realistic art, yet does not proceed from direct vision : as soon as a being feels under observation, naïve spontaneity of action is gone; consequently M. Degas does not copy from nature, he accumulates on the same subject a multitude of sketches, from which his work draws an irrefragable veracity. Never have pictures evoked less the painful image of a « model who is posing ». His colour is masterly — at one and the same time cunning and personal : he exteriorizes it on the turbulent medley of jockeys, on the ribbons and lips of dancing-girls. To-day he shows it by means of suppressed and as it were latent effects, the pretext of which is found in a shock of red hair, in the purplish folds of wet linen, in the pink of a hanging mantle, or in the acrobatic iridescence of circus-life. »

There also appeared in 1886 another good book — *Les Graveurs du XIXᵉ siècle,* by Henri Beraldi (Paris, L. Conquet), dealing with a special side of Degas' work, — his various essays in engraving, aquatint, dry-point, monotype, etc.

Having noted a very interesting fact for connoisseurs, « that these essays in engraving have often served the artist for the *groundwork* of his pastels », Beraldi writes as follows on the subject of Degas' monotypes, twenty-four of which we admired this year (March - April 1937) at the Degas Exhibition, in the Orangerie des Tuileries :

« Degas has several times amused himself by producing prints of a particular kind... A plate on which nothing is engraved is inked, and on this plate a drawing is made by removing the ink more or less. Then, under a press, a proof is obtained : a nocturnal or stage scene. The idea comes from a man of intelligence, and, as everyone knows, intelligence is not lacking in M. Degas. Proof of this is, that the uncompromising Degas tries his hand at uncompromising engraving. But are you aware of the prints which he looks at for his personal satisfaction? Well, nothing more nor less than the Mark Antonies. »

We are now sufficiently advanced in the career of Edgar Hilaire Germain Degas — the pupil of Lamothe and Ingres, the former student of the Ecole des Beaux-Arts, and who made his début at the Salon of 1865 with a pastel depicting *Une scène de guerre au moyen âge,* — to say that he is now recognized as one of the glories among the painters of the XIXth century in France. Not a single art critic can now deny that this renown is universal. His high qualities are sung in a multitude of books, pamphlets, art reviews and newspapers, whilst the artist keeps to himself more and more in order to meditate and work.

Here is what Gustave Geffroy wrote on Degas in an admirable notice in the third series of *La Vie artistique* (Paris, Dentu, 1894, pp. 147-180) :

« Degas is a Parisian... who has come to the right conclusion that to be an original artist he had no need either to change his situation by going to another country or to go back in time for subjects... Naturally he and his fellow-artists triumph to-day — those observers who have looked at Man as he is today, rustics who have lived with the peasants, who have traversed plains, woods and river-banks... The painters who will bequeath to the future a faithful image of their time seek for instruction elsewhere than among costumed lay-figures; they frequent the world, the line and colour of which they have an ambition to fix. They attach themselves not only to observing form and habits; they understand the spirit which animates everything. It is not on the table on which models stand that humanity passes before one. We must seek for it where it is... Degas has done this... And thus he has written that heart-rending, lamentable poem of the flesh, like a cruel observer who nevertheless loves life, like an artist enamoured of those great lines which envelop a figure from top to toe, like a savant who knows all about anatomy, the play of muscles, the twitching of nerves, the mottling and the thickness of the skin. »

Geffroy concludes his study by referring to the double life, as it were, of Degas :

« He has decided on two existences : one that of a passing and gay searcher, who goes hither and thither in the midst of social and artistic gatherings with an illusive smile and a witty remark; the other that of a recluse, in private with his models and sketches, working strenuously at the conjunction of tones and combinations of lines. He has thus accumulated his materials, heaped up an enormous documentation, composed a dictionary of details which would furnish, at the first evocation, the whole of a most rare and most personal piece of decorative work. — Nevertheless, there is nothing by Degas to be seen either at the Opéra or at the Hôtel de Ville in the way of decoration! »

Etienne Bricon's *Psychologie d'art — Les Maîtres de la fin du XIXe siècle* (Paris, L. Henry, May , 1900) brings us still nearer to today, when everybody is agreed on the subject of Degas' genius. He says in his study :

« M. Degas' vision is that of an Impressionist : wholly with his eyes... he stops what is in flight, he seizes and repeats it. We find the « don't move now ! » in his manner... Interesting himself in that way with life, M. Degas has set himself the task of recording its contemporary aspect; by looking about him he has delighted in the vulgar brutality which was the ugly characteristic of his day... Grappling with the twin maladies of our civilization — gallantry and low stage-life, he has selected victims wherever he could find them — in cafés, circuses, on the stage and behind the scenes. »

On the subject of the execution of his pastels, Bricon says that, thanks to the liberty of their style and the sureness of their planes, these works bring Degas singularly near to the great Japanese artists « whose lessons, in company, moreover, with all the Impressionists, he has followed... Japan, with its luminous and daring art, has had a powerful influence on our period »; an easy thesis to uphold when we remember the dry-points of Mary Cassatt, the pupil of Degas, and the works of Whistler.

We may also mention the fine pages by M. Georges Lecomte, in addition to the lengthy and penetrating study which M. Camille Mauclair devoted to Degas in the first book, published in 1903, on the « Maîtres de l'Impressionnisme ».

Among Degas' contemporaries abroad there are many critics whose writings it is well to read : Meier-Graefe, Müther, Thieme-Becker, Waldmann, J. B. Manson, and above all George Moore, who was half a Parisian, half an Englishman.

George Moore was superbly qualified to write about the painters of his epoch, since he lived among the Impressionists during the period of their struggle. The friend of Manet, Monet, Sisley, Pissarro and Degas, he has left many pages (like his friend Zola, Huysmans, Edmond and Jules de Goncourt and all the Naturalists in literature) on Degas and his art which are unforgettable (see *Confessions d'un jeune Anglais,* 1890, new edition 1925; *Modern Painting,* 1893; *Impressions and Opinions,* 1894), and his review articles, such as « Degas : The Painter of Modern Life », which appeared in the *Magazine of Art,* in 1890, are also worth unearthing. A single quotation is sufficient to prove that this contemporary recognized Degas' importance from the very beginning, for in his *Confessions,* one of his first books, which he wrote in French and published serially in Edmond Desjardins' review, he says :

« Cynicism was the great means of eloquence in the Middle Ages, and it is with cynicism that Degas has again made nudity an artistic possibility. What Mr. Horseley or the English matron will say it is difficult to guess. Perhaps hideous nature as painted by M. Degas will terrify her more than the sensuality they condemn in the case of Sir Frederick Leighton? »

No one ever thinks now of passing judgment on this « hideous » nature, and Degas appears definitely as a great classical painter, related to Clouet and Ingres, though advocates of academic art would have been the last to suspect it. It was, indeed, the evidence of his truly traditional and profound classicism which brought upon the old master a sort of disfavour — however without importance — on the part of the deforming Cubists or the more recent Expressionists, who inclined towards an « international art », — an « uprooted » art, — the first signs of which awakened in Degas his ironical disdain.

DETAILED DESCRIPTION

OF THE PLATES AND REPRODUCTIONS

33. SELF-PORTRAIT OF THE ARTIST. 1855. Canvas, 0,81 m. by 0,645 m. Musée du Louvre, Paris. Photo Hypérion.

34. A SELF-PORTRAIT. 1857. An etching, 0,23 m. by 0,142 m. Photo Floury.

35. PORTRAIT OF DEGAS AND THE PAINTER VALERNES. 1868. Canvas, 1,16 m. by 0,89 m. Musée du Louvre, Paris. Photo Arch. Phot. d'Art et d'Histoire.

36. HALF-LENGTH PORTRAIT OF A MAN. Canvas, 0,55 m. by 0,46 m. Private collection. Photo Durand-Ruel.

37. PORTRAIT OF HILAIRE DEGAS, THE ARTIST'S GRAND-FATHER. Canvas, 0,55 m. by 0,41 m. Musée du Louvre, Paris. Photo Arch. Phot. d'Art et d'Histoire.

38. PORTRAITS OF ALEXIS AND HENRI ROUART. Canvas, 0,92 m. by 0,73 m. Private collection. Photo Durand-Ruel.

39. PORTRAITS OF AUGUSTE DEGAS — THE ARTIST'S FATHER — AND THE GUITARIST PAGANS. Circa 1872. Canvas, 0,53 m. by 0,40 m. Musée du Louvre, Paris. Photo Arch. Photo d'Art et d'Histoire.

40. PORTRAIT OF DIEGO MARTELLI. 1879. Canvas, 0,75 m. by 1,15 m. Jacques Seligmann, Paris. Photo Hyperion.

41. A PORTRAIT GROUP : WALTER SICKERT, DANIEL HALÉVY, LUDOVIC HALÉVY, J. E. BLANCHE, GERVEX AND BOU-LANGER CAVE, Circa 1880. 1,15 m. by 0,71 m. Private collection. Photo Durand-Ruel.

42. PORTRAIT OF EUGÈNE MANET. Ernest Rouart, Paris. Photo Floury.

43. A WOMAN READING. Pastel. Private collection. Photo Durand-Ruel.

44. A YOUNG WOMAN WITH RED HAIR. 1870-1872. 0,43 m. by 0,52 m. Private collection. Photo Durand-Ruel.

45. HALF-LENGTH PORTRAIT OF A WOMAN. 1881-1882. Canvas, 0,405 m. by 0,325 m. Albert S. Henraux, Paris. Photo Durand-Ruel.

46. PORTRAIT OF A YOUNG WOMAN SEATED AGAINST A BACKGROUND OF CHRYSANTHEMUMS (Portrait said to be of Mademoiselle Malo). Canvas, 0,81 m by 0,65 m. Chester Dale, New York. Photo Durand-Ruel.

47. PORTRAIT OF MADEMOISELLE MALO. Circa 1869. Pastel, 0,46 m. by 0,38 m. J. E. Blanche, Paris. Photo Durand-Ruel.

48. PORTRAIT OF THE DUCHESSE DE MORBILLI, NÉE THÉ-RÈSE DEGAS (the artist's sister). Circa 1855-1856. Canvas, 0,89 m. by 0,67 m. Musée du Louvre, Paris. Photo Arch. Phot. d'Art et d'Histoire.

49. PORTRAIT OF MADEMOISELLE DOBIGNY. 1869. Panel, 0,305 m. by 0,265 m. Kunsthalle, Hamburg. Photo Hypérion.

50. PORTRAIT OF MADEMOISELLE SALLE. Drawing, 0,63 m. by 0,46 m. Madame Friedmann, Paris. Photo Floury.

51. HEAD OF A WOMAN. 0,31 m. by 0,24 m. Private collection. Photo Arch. Phot. d'Art et d'Histoire.

52. A WOMAN OF SAVOY. 0,615 m. by 0,46 m. Private collection. Photo Durand-Ruel.

53. PORTRAIT OF MADAME FÈVRE. 0,27 m. by 0,21 m. Musée du Louvre, Paris. Photo Floury.

54. THE BELLELI FAMILY. Circa 1860-1862. Canvas, 2 m. by 2,53 m. Musée du Louvre, Paris. Photo Arch. Phot d'Art et d'Histoire.

55. A STUDY OF HANDS FOR THE PORTRAIT OF THE BEL-LELI FAMILY (Plate 54). Circa 1860-1862. Canvas, 0,38 m. by 0,46 m. Musée du Louvre, Paris, Photo Arch. Phot. d'Art et d'Histoire.

56. PORTRAIT OF GIOVANNINA BELLELI. Canvas, 0,26 m. by 0,22 m. Musée du Louvre, Paris. Photo Arch. Phot. d'Art et d'Histoire.

57. STUDY FOR THE PORTRAIT OF THE BELLELI FAMILY (Plate 54). Cartoon on canvas, 0,46 m. by 0,30 m. Private collection. Photo Durand-Ruel.

58. A BEGGAR WOMAN IN ROME. 1857. 1,00 m. by 0,75 m. Mrs. Chester Beatty, London. Photo Durand-Ruel.

59. HEAD OF A YOUNG WOMAN. Circa 1862. Canvas, 0,27 m. by 0,22 m. Musée du Louvre, Paris. Photo Floury.

60. POUTING. Circa 1872-1873. Canvas, 0,32 m. by 0,46 m. Metropolitan Museum of Arts, New York. Photo Durand-Ruel.

61. THE CONVERSATION. Circa 1882. Pastel, 0,63 m. by 0,84 m. National Gallery, Berlin. Photo Durand-Ruel.

62. AN OLD ITALIAN WOMAN. Roma, 1857. 0,75 m. by 0,61 m. Private collection. Photo Durand-Ruel.

63. THE CONVERSATION. Pastel, 0,65 m. by 0,50 m. Private collection. Photo Durand-Ruel.

64. A WOMAN WITH A PINK HAT (PORTRAIT OF MADAME D. M.) 0,85 m. by 0,75 m. Private collection. Photo Durand-Ruel.

65. WOMAN IN A CAFÉ. Circa 1884. Panel, 0,65 m. by 0,46 m. Francis Salabert, Paris. Photo Hyperion.

66. PORTRAIT OF MADAME GOBILLARD-MORISOT. Circa 1865. Pastel, 0,485 m. by 0,305 m. Mlle Gobillard-Morisot. Ph. Floury.

67. THE DUCHESSE OF MONTEJASI-CICERALE WITH HER DAUGHTERS (Detail). Circa 1881. 0,66 m. by 0,98 m. D. David-Weill, Paris. Photo Arch. Phot. d'Art et d'Histoire.

68. YOUNG SPARTANS EXERCISING. 1860. Canvas, 1,10 m. by 1,545 m. Private collection. Photo Durand-Ruel.

69. THE RAPE OF THE SABINES (After Poussin). Canvas, 1,48 m. by 2,05 m, Marin-Bricka, Montpellier. Photo Floury.

70. THE MISFORTUNES OF THE CITY OF ORLEANS. 1865. Turpentine painting, 0,83 m. by 1,45 m. Musée du Louvre, Paris. Photo Arch. Phot. d'Art et d'Histoire.

71. SEMIRAMIS BUILDING A TOWN. 1861. Canvas, 1,48 m. by 2,55 m. Musée du Louvre, Paris. Photo Floury.

72. PORTRAIT OF MADEMOISELLE FIOCRE IN THE BALLET « LA SOURCE ». 1868. Canvas, 1,30 m. by 1,44 m. Metropolitan Museum of Art, New York. Photo Arch. Phot. d'Art et d'Histoire.

73. A COTTON BUREAU IN NEW-ORLEANS. 1873. Canvas, 0,74 m. by 0,92 m. Museum, Pau. Photo Floury.

74. TWO YOUNG WOMEN IN A PICTURE GALLERY. Canvas, 0,90 m. by 0,67 m. Private collection. Photo Durand-Ruel.

75. ABSINTHE. Circa 1876-1877. Canvas, 0,92 m. by 0,685 m. Musée du Louvre, Paris. Photo Floury.

76. A CAFÉ ON THE BOULEVARD MONTMARTRE. Circa 1877. Pastel, 0,42 m. by 0,60 m. Musée du Louvre, Paris. Ph. Floury.

77. AN INTERIOR SCENE (also entitled THE RAPE). Circa 1874. Canvas, 0,81 m. by 1,16 m. Henry Mac Ilhenny, Philadelphia. Photo Durand-Ruel.

78. A FALSE START. 0,32 m. by 0,41 m. Private collection. Photo Durand-Ruel.

79. A RACE COURSE STUDY. Circa 1882. 0,265 m. by 0,345 m. Private collection. Photo Durand-Ruel.

80. AT THE RACES. Pastel, 0,41 m. by 0,48 m. Private collection. Photo Durand-Ruel.

81. AT THE RACES (GENTLEMEN RIDERS). 1877-1880. Canvas, 0,665 m. by 0,82 m. Musée du Louvre, Paris. Photo Hypérion.

82. RACE-HORSES. 0,32 m. by 0,41 m. Private collection. Photo Durand-Ruel.

83. THE PARADE BEFORE THE GRAND STAND. Circa 1879. Turpentine painting on canvas, 0,46 m. by 0,61 m. Musée du Louvre, Paris. Photo Durand-Ruel.

84. CARRIAGE AT THE RACES. 1873. 0,36 m. by 0,55 m. Museum of Fine Arts, Boston. Photo Durand-Ruel.

85. AT THE RACES : BEFORE THE START. 1878. Canvas, 0,39 m. by 0,89 m. Mrs. Chester Beatty, London. Photo Durand-Ruel.

86. HOUSES AT THE BASE OF A CLIFF. Canvas, 0,92 m. by 0,73 m. Private collection. Photo Durand-Ruel.

87. MISS CASSATT IN A PICTURE GALLERY. Pastel on grey paper, 0,60 m. by 0,47 m. Henry Mac Ilhenny, Philadelphia. Photo Floury.

88. WOMEN DRESSING THEIR HAIR. Circa 1875-1876. Turpentine-painting on paper stuck on canvas, 0,31 m. by 0,45 m. Henry Lerolle. Photo Druet.

89. WOMAN AND CHRYSANTHEMUMS (Portrait of Madame Hertel). 1865. Paper stuck on canvas, 0,74 m. by 0,925 m. Metropolitan Museum of Art, New York. Photo Hyperion.

90. WOMAN DRESSING HER HAIR. A charcoal study completed with pastel, 0,60 m. by 0,44 m. Private collection. Photo Durand-Ruel.

91. THE TOILET. Circa 1885. Pastel, 0,65 m. by 0,495 m. Formerly Kelekian. Photo Druet.

92. A STUDY OF THE NUDE. 0,64 m. by 0,49 m. Formerly Bernheim Jeune, Paris. Photo Druet.

93. AFTER THE BATH. 1883. 0,53 m. by 0,33 m. Durand-Ruel. Paris. Photo Durand-Ruel.

94. AFTER THE BATH. Pastel, 0,52 m. by 0,38 m. Private collection. Photo Durand-Ruel.

95. THE PÉDICURE. 1873. Turpentine-painting on canvas. 0,61 m. by 0,46 m. Musée du Louvre, Paris. Photo Durand-Ruel.

96. BED-TIME. 0,37 m. by 0,27 m. Private collection. Photo Durand-Ruel.

97. AFTER THE BATH. Canvas, 1,16 m. by 0,95 m. Ambroise Vollard, Paris. Photo Hyperion.

98. A WOMAN IN HER BATH-TUB. Circa 1880. Pastel, 0,70 m. by 0,70 m. Private collection. Photo Durand-Ruel.

99. THE TOILET. Pastel, 0,60 m. by 0,61 m. Private collection. Photo Durand-Ruel.

100. AFTER THE BATH : A WOMAN DRYING HER FEET. Charcoal, 0,57 m. by 0,41 m. Private collection. Photo Durand-Ruel.

101. A STUDY OF THE NUDE. A charcoal drawing accentuated with pastel, 0,62 m. by 0,48 m. Private collection. Photo Durand-Ruel.

102. WOMAN IN HER BATH-TUB. Pastel, 0,60 m. by 0,83 m. Musée du Louvre, Paris. Photo Arch. Phot. d'Art et d'Histoire.

103. THE TOILET. Circa 1885-1886. Pastel, 0,72 m. by 0,585 m. Metropolitan Museum of Art, New York. Photo Durand-Ruel.

104. THE SONG OF THE DOG. 1876. Pastel. P. Rosenberg, Paris. Photo Floury.

105. A CAFÉ-CONCERT (« LES AMBASSADEURS »). Circa 1875. 1876. Pastel, 0,36 m. by 0,25 m. Museum, Lyons. Ph. Hyperion.

106. THE SINGER IN GREEN. 1884. Pastel, 0,60 m. by 0,45 m. Clark, New York. Photo Durand-Ruel.

107. A SINGER WITH A GLOVE. Circa 1880. Pastel, 0,54 m. by 0,46 m. Private collection. Photo Durand-Ruel.

108. WOMAN IRONING. 0,54 m. by 0,39 m. Private collection. Photo Durand-Ruel.

109. WOMAN IRONING. 1882. Canvas, 0,81 m. by 0,65 m. Durand-Ruel, Paris. Photo Durand-Ruel.

110. WOMEN IRONING. Canvas, 0,82 m. by 0,72 m. Schmitz, Dresden. Photo Durand-Ruel.

111. WOMEN IRONING. 1882. Canvas, 0,79 m. by 0,73 m. Durand-Ruel, Paris. Photo Durand-Ruel.

112. THE MILLINER. Pastel, 0,75 m. by 0,85 m. Private collection. Photo Durand-Ruel.

113. MILLINERS. Canvas, 0,76 m. by 0,82 m. E. Roche, Paris. Photo Hyperion.

114. A MILLINER'S WORK-ROOM. 1882. 0,485 m. by 0,70 m. Private collection. Photo Durand-Ruel.

115. PORTRAIT OF MADAME JEANTAUD LOOKING AT HERSELF IN A MIRROR. Canvas, 0,70 m. by 0,84 m. Mme Jacques Doucet, Paris. Photo Floury.

116. DANCING-GIRLS AT REST. Pastel, 0,50 m. by 0,60 m. Private collection. Photo Durand-Ruel.

117. WAITING. Circa 1880-1882. 0,47 m. by 0,60 m. Private collection. Photo Durand-Ruel.

118. DANCING-GIRL IN HER DRESSING-ROOM. Pastel, 0,66 m. by 0,50 m. Private collection. Photo Durand-Ruel.

119. DANCING-GIRLS ARRANGING THEIR TOILET. Circa 1878-1880. Pastel, 0,63 m. by 0,48 m. Private collection. Photo Durand-Ruel.

120. DANCING-GIRL IN HER DRESSING-ROOM. Circa 1874-1880. Pastel. Oskar Reinhart, Winterthur. Photo Floury.

121. DANCING-GIRLS BEHIND THE FRAMEWORK OF A FLAT. Painted in distemper and pastel, 0,69 m. by 0,48 m. Mrs. Edward Jonas, New York. Photo Hypérion.

122. THE DANCING-LESSON IN THE GREEN-ROOM. 0,45 m. by 0,60 m. Private collection. Photo Durand-Ruel.

123. THE DANCING-REHEARSAL. 0,47 m. by 0,61 m. Henri Rouart. Photo Durand-Ruel.

124. REST-TIME. Pastel, 0,75 m. by 0,55 m. Henri Rouart, Paris. Photo Durand-Ruel.

125. DANCING-GIRL AT THE PHOTOGRAPHER'S. 0,50 m. by 0,65 m. Private collection. Photo Durand-Ruel.

126. THE REHEARSAL IN THE GREEN-ROOM. Circa 1874-1875. 0,46 m. by 0,55 m. J. E. Blanche collection. Ph. Durand-Ruel.

127. REHEARSAL OF A BALLET ON THE STAGE. Circa 1874. Pastel, 0,534 m. by 0,73 m. Metropolitan Museum of Art, New York. Photo Durand-Ruel.

128. THE DANCING-LESSON. Circa 1874-1875. Pastel, 0,43 m. by 0,79 m. Private collection. Photo Durand-Ruel.

129. THE DANCING-LESSON. 1880-1885. Canvas, 0,38 m. by 0,88 m. Mrs. Esther Fiske Hammond, Santa Barbara, Calif. Photo Hyperion.

130. THE DANCING-LESSON WITH VIOLINIST. Circa 1882-1884. Pastel, 0,67 m. by 0,59 m. Private collection. Ph. Durand-Ruel.

131. MISS LALA AT THE FERNANDO CIRCUS (also called MISS LOLA). 1879. 1,17 m. by 0,78 m. Cawthra Mulock. Photo Durand-Ruel.

132. HALF-LENGTH STUDIES OF DANCING-GIRLS. Pastel, 0,72 m. by 0,70 m. Private collection. Photo Durand-Ruel.

133. HALF-LENGTH STUDIES OF DANCING-GIRLS. Charcoal drawing accentuated with white, 0,46 m. by 0,60 m. Private collection. Photo Durand-Ruel.

134. THREE DANCING-GIRLS. Pastel, 0,73 m. by 0,48 m. Private collection. Photo Durand-Ruel.

135. DANCING-GIRL RE-ARRANGING HER SHOULDER-STRAP. 0,45 m. by 0,35 m. Private collection. Photo Durand-Ruel.

136. RUSSIAN DANCING-GIRLS. Pastel, 0,67 m. by 0,48 m. Ambroise Vollard, Paris. Photo Hyperion.

137. HALF-LENGTH STUDIES OF DANCING-GIRLS. 1899. Pastel, 0,61 m. by 0,65 m. Museum of Art, Toledo, U.S.A. Photo Hyperion.

138. DANCING-GIRL IN GREEN. Pastel, 0,64 m. by 0,35 m. Private collection. Photo Durand-Ruel.

139. DANGING-GIRL. Pastel, 0,71 m. by 0,38 m. Private collection. Photo Durand-Ruel.

140. THE CLOSE OF AN ARABESQUE. Circa 1881. Pastel continued with oil-colours, 0,65 m. by 0,36 m. Musée du Louvre, Paris. Photo Floury.

141. DANGING-GIRL PIROUETTING. 0,45 m. by 0,35 m. Private collection. Photo Durand-Ruel.

142. THE BALLET. 1878. Pastel, 0,40 m. by 0,50 m. Private collection. Photo Durand-Ruel.

143. STARS OF THE BALLET. 0,365 m. by 0,49 m. Formerly Nemes collection. Photo Floury.

144. THE OPERATIC STAR. Circa 1876. Pastel, 0,58 m. by 0,42 m. Musée du Louvre, Paris. Photo Floury.

145. DANCING-GIRL THANKING HER AUDIENCE. 1877. Pastel on paper stuck on canvas, 0,75 m. by 0,78 m. Musée du Louvre, Paris. Photo Hyperion.

146. DANCING-GIRLS. 1879. Pastel, 0,48 m. by 0,64 m. Private collection. Photo Durand-Ruel.

147. ENTRANCE ON THE STAGE OF MASKED DANCERS. 1879. Pastel, 0,50 m. by 0,65 m. Private collection. Ph. Durand-Ruel.

148. TWO DANCING-GIRLS PRACTISING AT THE BAR. Charcoal, 0,45 m. by 0,58 m. Private collection. Photo Durand-Ruel.

149. DANCING-GIRLS PRACTISING AT THE BAR. 0,74 m. by 0,76 m. Metropolitan Museum of Art, New York. Photo Durand-Ruel.

150. THREE DANCING-GIRLS. A charcoal-drawing accentuated with pastel, 0,47 m. by 0,605 m. Bibliothèque Donat, Paris. Photo Durand-Ruel.

151. DANCING-GIRLS. A drawing accentuated with pastel, 0,47 m. by 0,60 m. Private collection. Photo Durand-Ruel.

152. DANCING-GIRLS. Pastel, 0,30 m. by 0,24 m. Private collection. Photo Durand-Ruel.

153. DANCING-GIRLS IN BLUE. Circa 1890. Canvas, 0,83 m. by 0,74 m. Dr. Albert Charpentier, Paris. Photo Hyperion.

154. A BALLET SCENE. 1878. Canvas, 0,25 m. by 0,20 m. Adolphe Lewisohn, New York. Photo Durand-Ruel.

155. MUSICIANS IN THE ORCHESTRA. 1872. Canvas, 0,69 m. by 0,20 m. Städtische Galerie, Francfort. Photo Durand-Ruel.

156. THE SUPERNUMERARIES. Pastel, 0,27 m. by 0,31 m. Musée du Louvre, Paris. Photo Floury.

157. REST-TIME. Circa 1893. Pastel, 0,50 m. by 0,65 m. Private collection. Photo Hyperion.

158. THE BOX. 1880. Pastel, 0,66 m. by 0,53 m. Paul H. Nitze, New York. Photo Durand-Ruel.

159. THE ORCHESTRA. Circa 1868. Canvas, 0,53 m. by 0,45 m. Musée du Louvre, Paris. Photo Arch. Phot. d'Art et d'Histoire.

160. THE BALLET OF « ROBERT LE DIABLE ». 0,66 by 0,55 m. Victoria and Albert Museum, London. Photo Durand-Ruel.

CONTENTS

PRINTED IN BELGIUM